T0115022

How to do your own BAS and save thousands in fees

Renelo Peque CPA

BALBOA.
PRESS

A DIVISION OF HAY HOUSE

Balboa Press books may be ordered through booksellers or by contacting:

Balboa Press
A Division of Hay House
1663 Liberty Drive
Bloomington, IN 47403
www.balboapress.com.au
1 (877) 407-4847

Because of the dynamic nature of the Internet, any web addresses or links contained in
this book may have changed since publication and may no longer be valid. The views
expressed in this work are solely those of the author and do not necessarily reflect the
views of the publisher, and the publisher hereby disclaims any responsibility for them.

Any people depicted in stock imagery provided by Thinkstock are models,
and such images are being used for illustrative purposes only.
Certain stock imagery © Thinkstock.

Printed in the United States of America.

ISBN: 978-1-4525-1241-9 (sc)
ISBN: 978-1-4525-1242-6 (e)

Balboa Press rev. date: 12/10/2013

Disclaimer

The information in this book does not constitute advice. The material in this publication has been derived from sources believed to be reliable and accurate such as www.ato.gov.au and www. fairwork.gov.au. It is of a general nature only and is not designed to take the place of a professional advice. While care has been taken in writing this book, the author, his practice Accounts Unplugged, the publisher and Renelo Peque Consulting Pty Ltd and its owners take no responsibility for its accuracy or completeness. Please seek competent professional advice before making any decision. The author makes no representation or warranty as to the reliability, accuracy or completeness of the information nor accepts responsibility arising in any way for errors in, or omissions from, the information. MYOB and Xero are separate accounting software companies and are the main software products used by the author and Accounts Unplugged.

Contents

THANK YOU

To my Creator – for the opportunity to make this contribution
to all business owners including my clients

To my family and friends –
with your support and encouragement
I was able to complete this book

Renelo Peque CPA

Chapter 1

What is this book about and why do you need it?

There are over two million small businesses that are actively trading in Australia as of June 2012, according to the Australian Bureau of Statistics. However, there are only 52,000 tax professionals in Australia including over 14,000 Business Activity Statements (BAS) agents and other professionals according to the Tax Practitioners' Board 2012 annual report. The ratio of BAS agents to the number of small businesses is negligible at *0.007*. It basically means that the number of BAS agents is not enough to service small businesses with their BAS compliance. The shortage of BAS agents will cause their fees to increase and many small business owners particularly those who are starting out will try not to incur these fees. As more small business owners try to save costs getting a BAS agent is at the bottom of the list. Or worse not on the list at all. This trend impacts the perception on BAS agents by small business owners and the value they provide. This book is an attempt to change that perception by educating and showing that there are many things involved towards preparing and lodging Business Activity Statements (BAS). This book also serves as a guide to those who want to manage the whole process involved in preparing and lodging Business Activity Statements (BAS) to save some BAS agent fees.

On the other end of the spectrum, there are business owners who wait until the last minute to get help. Or even worse some completely ignore anything tax related. Then they receive ATO notices and reminders that they do not attend to. A few weeks later they receive a letter from the ATO advising them of the penalty being charged. All these happened because of neglect. And your accountant cannot remind you all the time. As a business owner you control your business and that includes managing your books and tax deadlines. If you neglect your accounts, you will lose track on how your business is performing. You do not know if you are making money or not until one day you will realise that you cannot pay your suppliers because the sales that are coming in are not enough. You are suddenly on a hot seat and do not know what to do. Then you decide to get help. By then, it would be too late and the suppliers come knocking at your door. It is like driving a car without a thermostat until right in the middle of your journey, you notice some smoke coming out of your bonnet. A simple issue that could have been fixed but because of neglect resulted to more problems. Same as with a business, you are ultimately responsible for the accuracy of your business accounts.

Concept of 'safe harbour'

In tax administration there is a concept they call 'safe harbour,' where the taxpayer may not be liable to certain administrative penalties if they provide all the relevant tax information to the registered agent and that agent does not take reasonable care and makes a false or misleading statement that results in a shortfall amount or if the agent takes reasonable care or lacks reasonable care and fails to lodge the document by the due date. Safe harbour only applies to a false or misleading statement penalty and that statement was made on or after 1st of March 2010 or a failure to lodge on time penalty where the document has a due date for lodgement of 1st of March 2010 or later. For more information about safe harbour contact the ATO on 13 28 66 or check the ATO website. It is vital that business owners need to know and understand their rights as well as their obligations with their accounts and tax affairs. This book is not intended to replace BAS or tax advice nor does it contain exclusive information about Business Activity Statements as individual circumstances may vary. This book explains the basic concepts and practical ways you need to know about Business Activity Statements and what happens in practice. In this way, you will be able to adjust your existing ways of doing things or put a system in place if you do not have one in your business so that you capture the correct and complete information needed to be included and declared in your Business Activity Statements. This book will also show you to access tools from government websites, for example the Australian Taxation Office's small business assist website which is a great search tool that not many people know about.

The author is a partner of both MYOB and Xero online accounting. In our examples we use *MYOB AccountRight Plus Version 19.9* and *Xero* online accounting. The **'How to...'** chapters which are from 5 to 10 will be using screen prints and diagrams to assist you on how to actually do things in MYOB or Xero online accounting. In Chapter 4 we cover accounting software programs. The rest of the chapters will be mainly concepts and may use diagrams if necessary to facilitate comprehension. We also include practical tips on how to capture information that you need for your BAS reporting obligations. The idea is to have a mix of both theory and practice in all chapters as much as possible.

This is your first step towards educating yourself on how to keep your accounts in order. If you notice repeated information in some of the chapters it probably is. As what they say in professional development seminars, *'repetition is the mother of skill.'*

Economy and social trends

According to the Australian Bureau of Statistics, unemployment increased from 701,600 to 706,900 an increase of 5,300 in a month from June to July 2013. That's 176 jobs every day for 30 days. We hear massive job cuts at both big and small companies. Although as a whole it is not good for the economy, for some it is a blessing in disguise because they were inspired to start their own business.

Our societies underwent and are still undergoing transformation. The Agricultural Revolution continued until the end of the 19th century while the Industrial Revolution started in the late 18th century. The Industrial Revolution marked an unprecedented sustained growth that increased the living standards of the masses. Then the Second Industrial Revolution also called the Technical Revolution followed which was considered to have started in the 1860s. Then the Digital Revolution followed which marked the start of the Information Age. We are now in the age of social networking, mobile networked devices, cloud computing, smartphones and tablet computers. The businesses that are quick to adapt to these trends are the ones that will thrive better. We hear more online businesses being created. More and more start-ups and success stories grab the headlines. And as more new products and services are sold and bought, business processes and administration also need to evolve to take advantage of the benefits of increased productivity, efficiency and accuracy from the use of technology. As you decide to do your accounts yourself, ensure that you take advantage of the tools and support resources you need. In case of doubt ring the ATO. You can even try to tweet them on www.twitter.com. Inaccurate books can result to incorrect taxes. And incorrect taxes can result to fines, penalties and interest. All these can be prevented by keeping on top of things and organising your books. This starts with accurate and timely capture and recording of the business transactions rather than wait until the end of every quarter.

Attitude towards compliance and technology

Compliance does not start at the end of the quarter when you lodge your BAS. The process of tax compliance particularly with your BAS obligations starts from when the transactions occur and how accurately and timely you capture and record those transactions. Small business owners' time are spent on the daily operations and how to acquire more clients. Many of them also start to do their own books primarily to save accounting fees. Or some of them just cannot find the right or competent person. I know some bookkeepers themselves make mistakes on how they treat and record transactions because of lack of experience and complete understanding on the tax implications. Many of them are just not willing to put in the effort to learn the industry and how the business works and until you understand how the business works and how the transactions flow you may not be able to come up with more efficient ways on how to capture and record information. The pressure on efficiency and productivity these days increases more than ever as technology explodes to a phenomenal level. It becomes more accessible and affordable. This means that as a business owner you can directly access that technology without having a mediator or an accountant. Those who adopt the latest technology are the ones who will be on top of their game. If you do not take advantage of this technology your competitors will.

Shortage of BAS professionals

Tax and BAS professionals are administered and regulated by the Tax Practitioners Board (TPB) of Australia. There are minimum standards required on education and experience to be admitted as an agent. The profession is regulated to protect the public and to ensure that tax and BAS professionals provide quality services to clients. However, the shortage of qualified BAS professionals poses a dilemma. And that is whether business owners would pay thousands of fees for a BAS agent or to do it themselves to save thousands in fees to improve the bottom line. As technology these days becomes more accessible and affordable there is more reason for you to start preparing the BAS yourself and take control of your own finances.

Expensive accountants

Many still do not know the difference between a tax agent and a BAS agent. The Tax Agent Services Act (TASA) of 2009 lists the services called 'BAS services' that only a BAS agent can provide. A tax agent can provide more services than a BAS agent including BAS services which is why the fees are higher for a tax agent. You do not need to get a tax agent manage your books. A BAS agent can do this at a much lower price but still in the thousands of dollars every year. Ideally, the BAS agent needs to work closely with the tax agent and this does not always happen. Some tax agents prefer to use BAS agents who have understanding of the industries of their clients. But for whatever reason, every time the business owner attempts to get the BAS agent recommended by the tax accountant, something gets in the way – expensive fees, too much requirements by the BAS agent, location or perhaps the business owner just does not like how the BAS agent conducts its business. Most of the time, however, it is the expensive fees that mainly influence the decision to whether or not hire someone to do the books and prepare the BAS.

Most accounting professionals are affiliated with a national professional organisation of tax professionals like CPA Australia or ABN Tax. Having professional affiliations provide an excellent support system for its members. Those organisations require high professional standards for its members. The author's practice Accounts Unplugged is a CPA practice and as such holds a high degree of professional standard. We pass on the benefits to you as a reader by attempting to equip you with the basic knowledge on how to go about doing your own BAS with less or no errors.

Notes

Notes

Chapter 2

What is your business or industry?

<u>Overview</u>

A business in a particular industry may require a separate set of accounts although it can use a template chart of accounts already set up in an accounting system like MYOB for example. In the fashion and clothing industry, for example a T-shirt shop maintains an inventory account. It may sell different types and brands of shirts and to keep track of the movements that shop maintains a subsidiary ledger which is a detailed record of what product is sold, what is currently in stock and available for sale. Depending on how much detailed product information the owners want, the subsidiary ledger can be as detailed down to the brand, colour or size. On the other hand, professional service industry businesses like a law firm does not maintain an inventory account of products.

<u>Food industry</u>

One of the challenging industries in terms of the amount of work involved in maintaining the books is a food grocery shop or convenience food store. It is because it sells a mixture of small-sized GST taxable and GST free items. Products may be sold in small or big quantities at different times. Each type of food has various brands from various suppliers, ordered in different batches hence different expiry dates, different flavours, different sizes, different packaging, and so on. Those who maintain a manual system will have this issue. You will still need a cash register machine. In Chapter 6, we show you how to calculate your GST and GST-free transactions using your summary reports from your cash register. We also give you an overview of the easier options given by the ATO to account for your GST and GST-free transactions if you meet certain conditions. To give you some idea of what common items food shops normally have difficulty with when it comes to reconciling the books, the following are ATO examples of GST-free foods. Items not on the list are probably GST taxable.

- bread and bread rolls without icing or filling
- fats and oils for cooking
- milk, cream, cheese and eggs
- spices and sauces
- fruit juice containing at least 90% by volume of juice
- bottled drinking water
- tea and coffee (unless it is ready to drink)
- baby food and infant formula
- meat (except prepared meals or snacks)
- fruit, vegetables, fish and soup
- spreads, such as honey, jam and peanut butter
- breakfast cereals
- rice, cooked or uncooked (but not hot)

Although the item you sell may be on the GST-free list, it may still be taxable under certain circumstances. Bread rolls for example which are GST-free can be taxable when you sell them in a restaurant and customers eat them there.

To also give you an idea of the difference between GST-taxable and GST-free food items, below are examples of taxable items:

- biscuits, wafers, cones
- chocolates, lollies
- ice cream
- cakes, pastries and pies and other similar bakery products
- potato chips and other savoury snacks
- chocolate milk and other flavoured milk
- softdrinks
- food platters
- food marketed and sold as prepared meals such as sushi and rice dishes
- all food and drinks sold in restaurants or for consumption on the premises
- plants and seeds that grow into fruit and vegetables
- live animals and animal food

If you are unsure whether an item is taxable or not go to <u>www. ato.gov.au/Business/Consultation--Business/In-detail/Food-industry/Food-classification-for-GST/GST-food-guide</u>. This link is valid at the time of writing this book. Otherwise, you can google '*food guide GST ATO.*'

Many small business owners would only have a basic cash register with basic keys to choose from, such as GST sale or GST-free sale. Then at the end of the day, they print out a summary of the sales showing the amount of total sales and the GST amount. Different types of cash registers have different ways of set up so take time to read the manual. Ensure that you set it up correctly and include separate keys for GST sales, GST-free sales and Non-taxable. Every time you sell a product that has GST, you press the GST sale key and every time you sell a GST-free item you press the GST-free sale.

Food retailers may be eligible to use a simplified accounting method to estimate their sales and purchases that have both GST and GST-free components. The following are the ATO forms that you can download:

1. *Simplified GST accounting methods for food retailers* (NAT 3185)
2. *GST food guide* (NAT 3338)

The ATO is making it easier for small business owners by publishing guides and explanatory documents on their website. Make use of them because they were written for you. You can also use the tool website www.sba.ato.gov.au that the ATO developed for easy search of taxation terms and concepts.

Importation

When you buy materials overseas you incur freight costs, custom duties, quarantine fees, customs broker fees and GST on certain imported goods. Generally, you would use the services of an experienced customs broker who knows how to deal and coordinate with customs officers, shipping company and storage for your products. This process is critical because a single miscommunication can lead to your products not having a place for storage and if you have perishable or frozen food products you run the risk of them being spoiled. Once the whole process of bringing the products out of customs and into the storage facility is completed, the broker will send you an invoice detailing the costs it incurred. The invoice may also include amounts paid on your behalf that require reimbursement. Along with the invoice, the broker will attach the list of products that have been imported to Australia including those for which GST was paid. You can claim back through tax credits the GST that you paid for these imported products. This list from the broker will guide you on what items to charge GST on when you sell them.

Service industry

Maintaining your accounts for a service business is relatively straightforward. The revenues are mostly paid by cheque, cash or EFT. If you have employees to pay, there will be additional compliance with minimum wage, PAYG withholding, superannuation, payslips, among others. If you are unsure, you can ring the Australian Taxation Office and Fair Work Australia on how to go about setting up and maintaining your own payroll. The author is also working on his second book on how to process payroll including concepts and practices in the industry. That book will also show how to process your own payroll using MYOB and Xero online accounting.

Peculiarities of each industry

Each industry has its own unique set of accounts but once those accounts are set up correctly, the other common accounts are relatively easy to set up. For example, a grocery shop which is in the category of food industry maintains an inventory account which is not used in a professional service industry. MYOB has templates of accounts you can choose for different types of businesses.

GST overview

Not all expenses have GST on them. As explained before, many food items are GST-free. There are also transactions or supplies that are input-taxed such as interest on investments and rent on residential properties. In Chapter 10, we summarise the items that are included at each label of the Business Activity Statement (BAS). That is the chapter that you want to spend more time on. You may want to refer to that chapter once in a while with what to include or exclude on your BAS as you progress through the chapters. Before you start entering transactions in MYOB, determine whether the item has GST or not by either confirming with the supplier as shown on the invoice given to you. You also want to check on www.abr.gov.au whether the supplier is registered for GST or not. Only those who are registered can charge GST on supplies. More importantly, you need to check your own GST registration status including the effective date. Ensure that when you reach or expect to reach the GST turnover threshold that you register.

Recording transactions not according to the accounting method you advised the ATO will create issues. For example, if you are registered to use the Accrual method, sales are recorded and included in your BAS when the invoices are issued even when payment has not yet been received. If you forget to take this accounting method into account your BAS figures will be incorrect and may affect your subsequent BAS. Goods and services tax (GST) ruling GSTR 2000/13 provides more information when you choose to account on a cash basis. It outlines the things that the ATO will consider to determine if it is appropriate for you to account for GST on a cash basis. If you are not eligible to account for GST on a cash basis, you must account on a non-cash-basis (accrual) unless the ATO gives you approval to use cash basis.

You are eligible to account for GST on a cash basis if you meet any of the following:

- You are a small business with an annual turnover of less than $2 million. This includes related entities
- You are carrying on an enterprise with a GST turnover of $2 million or less
- You use cash basis for income tax

- You carry on a kind of enterprise that the ATO worked out to be capable of being accounted on a cash basis regardless of turnover
- You are one of the following:

> Endorsed charitable institution
> Trustee of an endorsed institution
> Gift-deductible entity
> Government school

Note that although you are not in any of the above category you can still apply with the ATO to use cash basis. Ring 13 28 66 for more information.

Just a quick overview on how to check you GST summary figures: if you are using MYOB print out the GST report in MYOB using the Accrual by going to:

Reports>GST/Sales Tax>GST [Summary – Accrual]

When you run this report, it will default to 'All' for both tax codes and card type. Ensure that the date range is for the period of the BAS that you are lodging. Then click 'Display.'

The report below shows the summary of the total sales and purchases values both with GST and GST-free. It also shows the tax collected that relates to the GST sales and tax paid that relates to the purchases. The report also shows the non-taxable (N-T) sales and purchases. These non-taxable (N-T) items do not go to the BAS at all because they are not taxable. Examples are superannuation, advances or loans to associates and drawings.

Clearwater Pty Ltd
123 One Street
Box Hill
VIC 3128

GST [Summary - Accrual]

1/07/2013 To 30/09/2013

6/11/2013 12:19:59 AM						Page 1
Code	Description	Rate	Sale Value	Purchase Value	Tax Collected	Tax Paid
ABN	No ABN Withholding	(48.500%)		$810.38		-$764.00
CAP	Capital Acquisitions	10.000%		$1,500.00		$136.36
FRE	GST Free	0.000%		$1,276.75		
GST	Goods & Services Tax	10.000%	$19,983.50	$41,113.12	$1,816.66	$3,737.55
N-T	Not Reportable	0.000%	$26.80	$142.89		
				Total:	$1,816.66	$3,109.91

Diagram 2.1 GST [Summary – Accrual] report in MYOB

If you prefer to go through the transactions that have GST or not, you can generate the detailed version of that GST report via the same path *Reports>GST/Sales Tax>* and select *GST [Detail – Accrual]* if you use the Accrual method or *GST [Detail – Cash]* if you use the Cash method. By generating the detailed version of the GST report you will be able to review each line of transaction. When you click on a line, it will bring you to the entry if you want to amend it. Hover your cursor on a line until it changes to a magnifying glass. Note that there are four types of GST reports you can generate: GST Summary-Accrual, GST Summary-Cash, GST Detail-Accrual and GST Detail-Cash. The path again for the detailed GST accrual method report is:

Reports>GST/Sales Tax>GST Detail – Accrual

Tax codes exception

MYOB has Tax Code reports that you can run to check that correct tax codes were used. For example, you can use the report Tax Code Exceptions (Cash transactions) if you want to check what tax code was used for a transaction recorded as *Spend Money* in Banking. In our example below, the Bank Charges account was recorded using the tax code GST for $33.64 and N-T for $47.89 but the default code of this account was set up as FRE (GST free). Do not worry about recording at this chapter. Expense recording is in Chapter 5. These checks are highlighted now so you know what to watch out for when you start the recording process in Chapter 5.

Clearwater Pty Ltd
123 One Street
Box Hill
VIC 3128

Tax Code Exceptions [Cash Transactions]

1/07/2013 To 30/09/2013

6/11/2013 12:22:46 AM						Page 1
Date	ID#	Name	Account Name	Default Code	Entered Code	Amount
1/07/2013	107	The Best Technologies Pty L	Computer Equipm	N-T	CAP	$1,363.64
30/07/2013	SC300701	Bank Charges	Bank Charges	FRE	GST	$33.64
31/07/2013	GJ000001	To record dep'n of photocopi	Depreciation	GST	N-T	$37.50
30/08/2013	SC300801	Bank Charges	Bank Charges	FRE	N-T	$47.89

Diagram 2.2 Tax Code Exceptions [Cash Transactions] report in MYOB

Below is the diagram that shows the setup of 6-1130 Bank Charges account. Note that it is set up with a tax code of FRE (GST free). This means that every time you use this account for a transaction, it will default to FRE (GST-free) unless you manually change it.

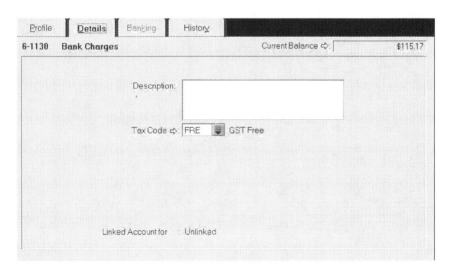

Diagram 2.3 Tax-code details of the Bank Charges account in MYOB

We can see in our example that when the bank charges transaction was recorded on 30/07/13, it was incorrectly coded to GST. Bank charges generally are GST-free except for other products or services like EFT merchant fees which attract GST. The transaction for 30/08/13 was also incorrectly recorded as N-T (not taxable). To correct this, just hover your cursor on the line in the Tax Code Exceptions (Cash transactions) report until it changes to a magnifying glass then click it. It will bring you to the original entry made that you can amend. Our example below shows that the journal entry has been reconciled. Just click [OK] and update the tax code to FRE (GST-free) by clicking on the blue arrow next to the tax code GST. It will then give you a list to pick the tax codes from. Choose FRE (GST-free) and click [OK].

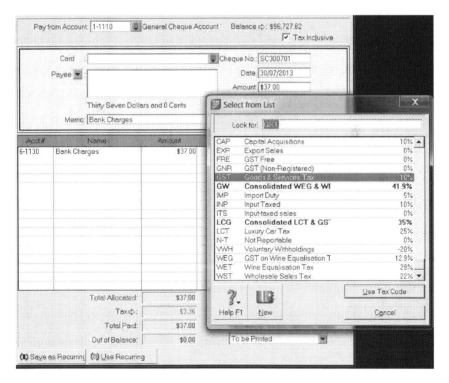

Diagram 2.4 Changing the tax code of an entry in MYOB

Another tax report that you can use is the Tax Code Exceptions (Invoice Transactions) report. As opposed to the previous Tax Code Exceptions (Cash Transactions) which highlights the exceptions from the *Spend Money* section of the *Banking* menu in the Command Centre, this report is for the transactions that were processed in *Purchases* menu. Generally, normal purchase transactions relating to your daily operations are entered via *Purchases*. To review and correct, follow the same approach we just did for the bank charges.

ATO website and Accounts Unplugged resources

Remember the ATO website is your friend. It has been updated in 2013 that produced a much better navigation and modern look and feel. If you search something in the internet about BAS and tax try to include the word 'ATO' as part of your search key words so that the relevant ATO pages will come up rather than some random websites. When you process your own BAS, try to use government sites for resources and if possible, save a copy of the pages that you are basing your decision on. Save them in the folder where the relevant income or expense documents are also saved.

If all information about tax, BAS and accounting are available online for free, what is stopping you to learn about BAS which is another business skill? And even if you currently have an accountant or bookkeeper doing your books, by educating yourself you will know what questions to ask. Eventually, the more education you get about BAS, the more you will gain confidence. But you will need to make that decision. As the number of BAS professionals per business in Australia is negligible at *.007*, plus the fact that their fees are expensive it is necessary for you to learn the basic skills to equip you to prepare and lodge your own BAS to save thousands in fees. You can also opt to subscribe to our Q&A online support called BAS accountant online on our website <u>www.</u>

accountsunplugged.com. As we endeavour to support as many small business owners through this Q&A online service, there is a 48-hour response time. Depending on the volume and complexity of queries you may receive a response in less than 48 hours.

Notes

Notes

Chapter 3

BAS-related obligations and other business matters

Process diagram of BAS compliance

One of the most efficient ways of complying with your BAS obligations is having a system or two in place where you do not have to think about what to do. The way to do this is to have a checklist, a good accounting system that automates some of the tasks and a support system in case you need help. Support systems can be the ATO on 13 28 66 or www.ato.gov.au or BAS accountant online on www. accountsunplugged.com You can ring the ATO on 13 28 66. You can also subscribe to our BAS accountant online at www. accountsunplugged.com.

Diagram 3.1 Process overview of the record-keeping and BAS compliance process

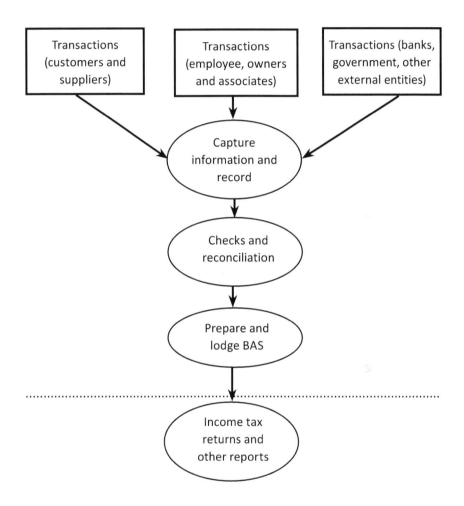

ABN registration

The Australian Business Number or ABN is a unique number issued to a business by the government through the Australian Business Register (www.abr.gov.au). You are not required to have a Tax File Number (TFN) to apply for ABN but the processing may be delayed if you do not provide your TFN. You quote this number in your dealings with customers, suppliers, government agencies, banks, and other entities. Technically, ABN registration is not mandatory which means a business can trade without an ABN. However, the business that deals and pays you is required to withhold 46.5% if the ABN is not quoted. So you are better off having an ABN. When you deal with entities like a bank you will probably need an ABN anyway.

You are entitled to an ABN if you are a company registered under the Corporations Law in Australia, an entity that is carrying on an enterprise in Australia or a government entity. A non-resident entity may also be entitled to an ABN if it is carrying on an enterprise in Australia or in the course of carrying on an enterprise; it makes supplies that are connected with Australia. The best way to apply for an ABN is online at www.abr.gov.au. You can also get a tax agent to lodge it for you electronically. You can still use paper application but you will have to order the forms depending on what entity it is for – sole, partnerships, company, trust or superannuation. You can order the forms online on http://business.iorder.com.au/ or phone 1300 720 092. Note that the form codes are NAT 2938 for sole traders; NAT 2939 for companies, partnerships, trusts and other organisations; and NAT 2944 for superannuation entities. ABN is registered per entity not business activity. For example, if you own a convenient store and also catering service, one ABN covers these activities. When a structure is in place where a company does the operations while a trust owns the building in which the operations occur each entity structure will need to be registered with a separate ABN.

Licenses and permits

Applying for an ABN is separate from applying for a business name, trademark or license. Business name registration is now administered by the Australian Securities and Investments Commission (ASIC) under the new National Business Names

Registrations System. This has replaced the states and territory registers and you only need to register once and it is registered nationally. Check the availability of the business name you would like to have at www.asic.gov.au before you can submit your application. You can also check our simple business setup guide at our website www.accountsunplugged.com.

Depending on which industry, licenses and permits are generally applied at your local council. For example in Melbourne, if you handle, prepare, package, store, serve, supply and repackage food, Food Act 1984 requires you to register with the local council. And if you are in the liquor business, the licensing requirements are administered by the Victorian Commission for Gambling and Liquor Regulation. The requirements for registration are on www.vcglr.vic.gov.au. The best place to start if you are not sure about licenses and permits for your business is www.business.gov.au. If you need to talk to them you can ring them on 1800 777 275 or use their live chat service on their website.

Copyrights, trademarks, patent and other intellectual properties

In Australia, the moment the idea is documented either on paper or electronically, it is automatically protected by copyright. That is why there is no government registry or application process for it. But remember that this copyright protection applies to original expression of ideas and not the ideas themselves. Works that are commonly protected are music, books and magazines, films and other artwork. Depending on the type of material, a copyright generally lasts 70 years from the year of the death of the author or from the year of the first publication after the death of the author. If you want to know more about copyrights go to the government's IP Australia website on www.ipaustralia.gov.au. IP stands for intellectual property.

If you want to distinguish the goods or services that you sell you may want to consider applying for a trademark. A trademark is a right given to a word, phrase, number, logo or image or even a letter so you have the exclusive right to use it commercially. It also includes the right to license or sell it for the goods and services associated with that right. IP Australia provides excellent guidance on how to go about a trademark application on their website.

A patent is a legally enforceable right given to the owner for any method, process or device that is new and useful. It is granted to give exclusive right mainly for commercial purposes. To check whether patent is right for you, go to the IP Australia website and it will guide you on how to go about the application process.

The best place to start if you have questions on intellectual properties is www.ipaustralia.gov.au and not a lawyer who will charge you before you even fill out an application. You can ring IP Australia on 1300 65 1010 or email at assist@ipaustralia.gov.au. They are also on Facebook, LinkedIn and YouTube.

GST registration

Registration for GST is mandatory if your turnover is $75,000 or more ($150,000 or more if you are a non-profit organisation). If you are in the taxi travel business your GST registration is mandatory regardless of your turnover. The turnover for GST purposes is the gross business income excluding GST (either actual or expected) for any 12-month period. You can apply for GST online through your business portal. You can also get your BAS agent or tax agent to do it for you. You can still apply using the paper form but you will need the form code number when you request for them. The forms are the same as the forms used for the ABN registration except for the superannuation. They are again

NAT 2938 for sole traders; NAT 2939 for companies, partnerships, trusts and other organisations. If you already have an ABN you can use NAT 2954 to register for GST.

PAYG withholding

Applying for PAYG withholding is also through www.abr.gov.au where you apply for ABN. You can actually apply for PAYG at the same time as you apply for ABN using the same form. If you have an ABN and would like to add a PAYG withholding account, you can also do it online at www.abr.gov.au. If you are not required to have an ABN but need to withhold from a payment you can submit an application to register a PAYG withholding account. Download the form NAT 3377 from the ATO website on instructions on how to apply. Once your application is granted you will be issued with a withholding payer number or WPN. This can be done using an Administrator AUSkey. An alternatively quicker way is to apply online through the business portal on https://bp.ato.gov.au/. You will need an AUSkey to use this portal. Below is a quick overview on how to apply for an AUSkey. If you want to save time on communicating with the ATO including lodgements of forms and submitting application. Getting the AUSkey and setting up your business portal credentials may take a little time but once it's done you can do almost all your ATO related dealings through the portal. To apply for an AUSkey which is your single key to access government online services go to www.abr.gov.au/auskey. There will be two options which are either to log in or to register. Click on the register option to apply for the AUSkey and follow the prompts. You will need your ABN and the name of the person to be listed as an associate of the business. If you have issues or doubts on applying for an AUSkey, phone 13 28 66. At the end of the application there should be a number that you can ring in case you get stuck. You can install the AUSkey on your computer,

USB stick or server. If you are the Administrator AUSkey holder you have options to:

- register other people for AUSkeys
- view AUSkeys
- update and cancel AUSkey associated with your business

Fringe benefits tax

A fringe benefit is a benefit provided to an employee or the employee's associate because that person is an employee. The person can also be a former or a future employee. The benefits can be provided by the employer, associate of the employer or a third party under an arrangement with the employer. Fringe benefits tax is paid by employers on certain fringe benefits as a result of the person's employment. FBT is a tax paid by the employer not the employee. FBT is calculated based on the taxable value of the fringe benefits.

The FBT you pay as an employer can generally be claimed as an income tax deduction. Check with your tax accountant or ring the ATO on 13 28 66.

Wine equalisation tax

This tax is a value-based tax on wine that is consumed in Australia. The WET rate is 29% of the before GST value at the last wholesale price which is called 'assessable dealings.' So if you are a wine producer, wholesaler or importer of wine, you normally have to pay WET. It only applies to those with alcohol content of over 1.15%. If you are wine producer you may be able to claim wine producer rebate. This amount will be pre-printed on you BAS if you have chosen Option 3. In this case you do not need to complete the Wine equalisation tax (WET) part of the

BAS. However, you still need to report WET payable (1C) and WET refundable (1D) when lodging your Annual GST return.

Luxury car tax

Luxury car tax (LCT) applies to a supply of luxury car if the following conditions exist:

- you make the supply in the course of your enterprise
- you make the supply in connection with Australia
- you are registered or required to be registered for GST

Supply under LCT is a sale by a dealer that sells a car to an individual or business, to a Commonwealth, state or territory agency or the sale or trade-in of a car.

Luxury car tax (LCT) is paid at the time you supply a luxury car unless the purchaser quotes their ABN to the seller in an approved format in which case the payment of LCT can be deferred until the car is sold or imported at the retail level. Generally you can quote your ABN if:

- you are registered for GST, and
- you have an ABN, and
- you intend to hold the car for trading stock (other than holding it for hire or lease); or carrying out research and development for the manufacturer of the car; or exporting the car where the export is GST-free under the GST law.

You will need to quote your ABN at or before the time of your purchase or importation of the luxury car not after buying the car. This does not however prevent you from claiming an adjustment on your BAS if you were entitled to quote your ABN and registered for both LCT and GST. You can use the following format when you quote your ABN:

I hereby quote Australian Business Number _____
in relation to the supply of the luxury car as detailed
attached:

Name of business:
_____

Name of person authorised to quote:
_____

Signature of person authorised to quote:
_____

Date: _____

The attachments need to include the order for the luxury car or any other document provided to the supplier or the Australian Customs and Border Protection Service.

If you buy a luxury car for a non-quotable purpose, you need to tell the supplier that the luxury car is to be used for a non-quotable purpose before purchasing it, otherwise you will need to account this on your BAS as an increasing change of use adjustment. You can use the following format:

I hereby notify you that I am not quoting Australian Business Number _____ ***for the supply of the following luxury car:***

Description of car:

_____

Date of transaction:

_____

Signature of person authorised to quote:

_____

Australian Business Number:

_____

Name of business:

_____

Name of person authorised to make this declaration:

_____

Signature:

_____

Date: _____

There are also other situations when luxury car tax does not apply other than quoting the ABN:

- the car is more than two years old which means it was manufactured in Australia more than two years before the supply; or

- the car was imported and entered for home consumption more than two years before the supply
- the car is exported as a GST-free export

When entering a luxury car for home consumption you need to:

- complete the approved Australian Customs and Border Protection Service forms; or
- provide the Australian Customs and Border Protection Service with a quotation like the following:

I hereby quote my Australian Business Number _____
in relation to the importations described on the entry lines where I have indicated my intention to quote.

Note that the person authorised to quote the ABN depends on the type of entity. It is generally the individual owner if it is a sole proprietorship, one of the partners if it's a partnership, the trustee if it is a trust or the public officer if it is a company.

PAYG instalment

Pay As You Go (PAYG) instalment system for expected income tax liability. The income can either be from business or investments. At the end of the year when your income is assessed, the amount you have paid to date will be credited to your tax liability to work out if there's a refund or more tax owing. The ATO uses your previous tax return to estimate tax liability. Generally those who earn $2000 or more will be notified of the instalment unless the latest notice of assessment is less than $500; or if the notional tax is less than $250; or if you are entitled to a senior's or pensioner's tax offset. Companies get notified if their instalment rate is more than 0%; or if notional tax is more than $250. Those companies that have $2 million in business and investment income pay using the instalment rate option.

When the ATO calculates the estimate tax liability it takes into account the likely growth in your business and investment income based on the GDP. The ATO will advise you how often you will make the payments on your BAS.

BAS reporting and payment options

Mandatory reporting and payment:

If your turnover is $20 million or more, you must report and pay GST monthly. The labels to be reported are:

- G1 (total sales)
- G2 (export sales)
- G3 (other GST-free sales)
- G10 (capital purchases)
- G11 (non-capital purchases)
- 1A (GST on sales)
- 1B (GST on purchases)

Other options:

If you report quarterly and pay GST quarterly, you can choose either option 1 or 2. The BAS will have a label next to each of the options. To indicate which option you like place an 'X' in the label.

If you are eligible to elect option 3, your BAS will contain a pre-printed instalment amount at G21.

Option 1 – Calculate, report and pay GST quarterly

Under this option, the following are the labels that need to be reported:

- G1 (total sales)
- G2 (export sales)
- G3 (other GST-free sales)
- G10 (capital purchases)
- G11 (non-capital purchases)
- 1A (GST on sales)
- 1B(GST on purchases)

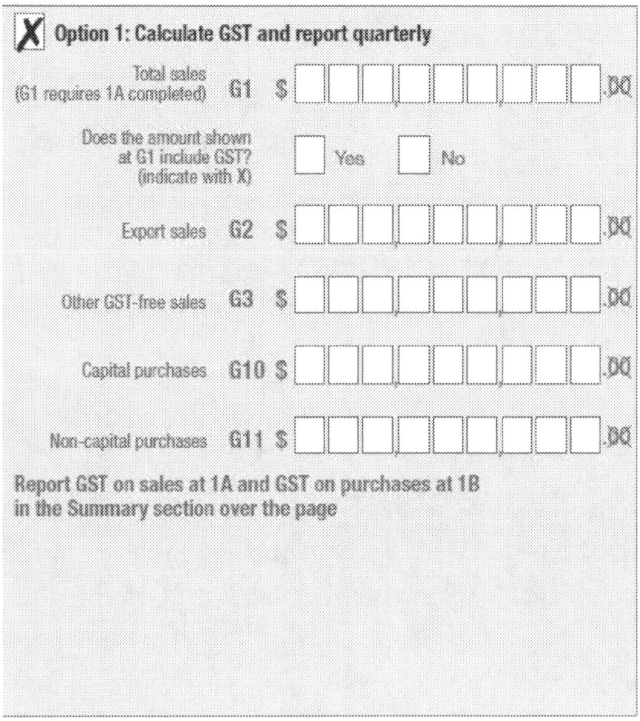

X Option 1: Calculate GST and report quarterly

Total sales
(G1 requires 1A completed) **G1** $ [ ][ ][ ][ ][ ][ ][ ][ ][ ].00

Does the amount shown
at G1 include GST?
(indicate with X) [ ] Yes [ ] No

Export sales **G2** $ [ ][ ][ ][ ][ ][ ][ ][ ][ ].00

Other GST-free sales **G3** $ [ ][ ][ ][ ][ ][ ][ ][ ][ ].00

Capital purchases **G10** $ [ ][ ][ ][ ][ ][ ][ ][ ][ ].00

Non-capital purchases **G11** $ [ ][ ][ ][ ][ ][ ][ ][ ][ ].00

Report GST on sales at 1A and GST on purchases at 1B
in the Summary section over the page

Diagram 3.2 Option 1 on your BAS

Option 2 – Calculate and pay GST quarterly and report annually

Under this option, you must report amounts at the following labels on your activity statement each quarter:

- G1 (total sales)
- 1A (GST on sales)
- 1B (GST on purchases)

At the end of the financial year the ATO will send you an Annual GST information report, on which you must report amounts at the following labels:

- G2 (export sales)
- G3 (other GST-free sales)
- G10 (capital purchases)
- G11 (non-capital purchases

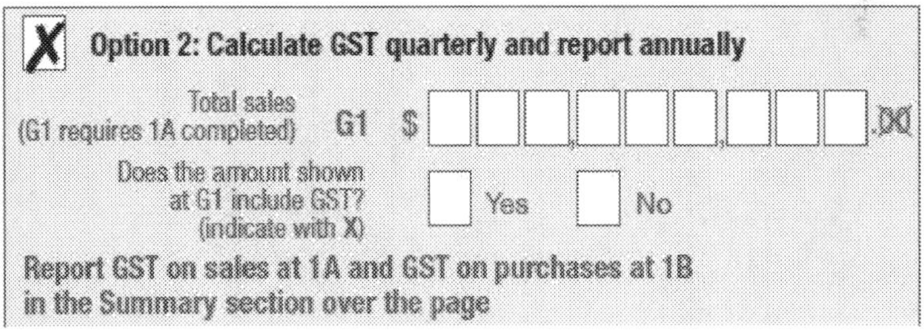

Diagram 3.3 Option 2 on your BAS

Option 3 – Pay a GST instalment amount quarterly and report annually

Under this option, you must pay a GST instalment amount worked out by us (or varied by you) each quarter (or twice-yearly in special cases). At the end of the financial year the ATO will send you an *Annual GST return*, on which you must report amounts at the following labels:

- G1 (total sales)
- G2 (export sales)
- G3 (other GST-free sales)
- G10 (capital purchases)
- G11 (non-capital purchases)
- 1A (GST on sales)
- 1B (GST on purchases)

The Annual GST return will also be used to account for any difference between your actual annual GST liability and the total of your instalment amounts for the year.

Report and pay GST annually

You can only use this option if you are voluntarily registered for GST. That is, you are registered for GST and your turnover is under $75,000 ($150,000 for non-profit bodies).

If you are eligible and have elected to report and pay GST annually, you do not need to report or pay any GST during the year. At the end of the financial year, you must report and pay any amount due. You must complete the following labels on your *Annual GST return*:

- G1 (total sales)
- G2 (export sales)
- G3 (other GST-free sales)
- G10 (capital purchases)
- G11 (non-capital purchases)
- 1A (GST on sales)
- 1B (GST on purchases)

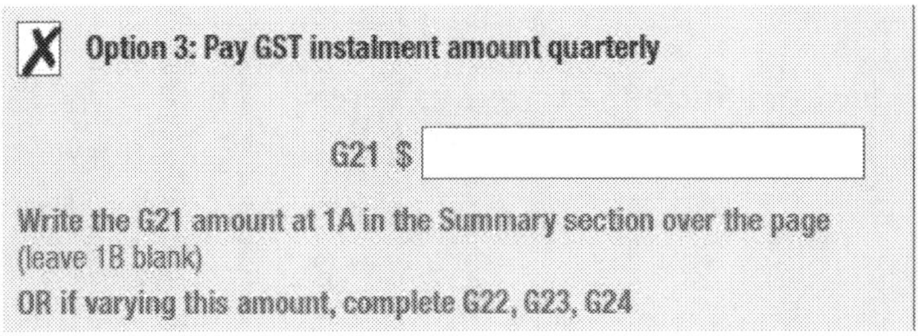

Option 3: Pay GST instalment amount quarterly

G21 $ [   ]

Write the G21 amount at 1A in the Summary section over the page
(leave 1B blank)
OR if varying this amount, complete G22, G23, G24

Diagram 3.4 Option 3 on your BAS

Below is the summary table of the three BAS options that you can
choose. There are certain labels that are added or used at each option.

OPTION 1 CALCULATE AND REPORT QUARTERLY	OPTION 2 CALCULATE QUARTERLY REPORT ANNUALLY	OPTION 3 PAY INSTALMENT AMOUNT AND REPORT ANNUALLY
G1	G1	
G2		
G3		
G10		
G11		
		G21 ATO instalment amount
		If varying, estimated net GST for the year
		If varying, G23 varied amount for the quarter
		If varying, G24 reason code for variation
1A GST on sales or GST instalment	1A GST on sales or GST instalment	1A GST on sales or GST instalment
1B GST on purchases	1B GST on purchases	

Diagram 3.5 BAS options table summary

Income tax

How to lodge your income tax return depends on the type of business entity. For sole traders it is relatively straightforward as your taxable income or loss is reported on the individual tax return. Partnerships also lodge a partnership return but that is only to report the net income or loss. Each individual partner lodges a tax return to report their share of the partnership income or loss. Any other assessable income is also reported on the return. The trust also reports the income or loss on a trust tax return. If you are the beneficiary of the trust, you report the income received from the trust as well as other assessable income. A company also lodges its own company tax return separate from the income of the directors or shareholders.

At the time of this book's writing in October 2013, the Australian Taxation Office was working on what is called 'push returns' to simplify and reduce the burden on individuals who have simple tax affairs. To make this happen, the ATO software used to submit tax returns called e-tax is to be reduced to 10 screens from 140. It will take approximately 25 minutes to complete this 'push return.'

Superannuation

It is an arrangement which people make to have funds available for them by the time they retire. Before 1992, there were superannuation arrangements in place under industrial awards. Currently, superannuation contribution rate is 9.25%. This rate is set to increase to 12% gradually by 2020. Generally, superannuation guarantee payments are required from those aged between 18 and 69 years old who earn $450 or more. Those who are under the age of 18 who work more than 30 hours per week earning $450 are also eligible. As at 1 July 2013, superannuation will be paid even if you're already 70. There is no more upper age limit.

The superannuation payment cut-off dates are 28 days after the end of each quarter. This means you make four payments a year. For example, for the July-September quarter, the payment cut-off is October 28. Employers can generally claim a tax deduction for superannuation contributions as company or business expense. Please consult your tax accountant regarding this.

The author is also working on a book on how to process your own payroll which includes a chapter on superannuation. The book is expected to be released in 2014. You can subscribe to our mailing list on our website for updates on this book.

Social Media

Government departments and agencies are on social media these days. For example, I follow the Australian Taxation Office on www.twitter.com and I receive regular tweets from them about updates on tax legislation, items that taxpayer can claim, superannuation, things that business owners need to know and a whole lot of other taxation concepts and updates. They also have a YouTube channel where they show videos on how to how do your e-tax for example and updates on superannuation in 2013. I particularly like following the ATO on Twitter as regular tweets (limit of 140 characters every tweet) enable me to absorb small chunks for information at a time. If you are not yet on social media, consider joining either Twitter or Facebook to get tax and legislation updates from the Australian Taxation Office, Fair Work and other government departments.

Notes

Notes

Chapter 4

Accounting software packages and online accounting

Online or cloud accounting

Cloud or online accounting is managing your accounts using the internet which is accessible anytime, anywhere. Below are some of the benefits of online accounting:

	Traditional accounting software	Online accounting
Data update	Updates data file only when done in the computer where the software is installed	Real-time, updates data file wherever or whenever data is entered
Backup	Regular backup	No need to do backups
Access	You need to have the computer where the software is installed	Anytime, anywhere
Security	Anyone can access the computer where the software is installed if not password-protected	Only accessible to those with access rights

Software and tax updates	Need to install and pay extra for updates including tax tables	Software updates done automatically including tax tables included in monthly subscription fee
Bank feeds	No bank feeds therefore delay in feeding data into the software	Bank feeds can be set up so that transactions are fed to software automatically
Productivity	No real productivity benefits	Improves productivity
Cost	High upfront software cost plus bookkeeper fees plus upgrade and updates costs	Affordable fixed monthly subscription
BAS (Business Activity Statement)	BAS link needs to be set up	Updates BAS figures upon transaction entry
Reports	Fixed standard reports	Customisable reports
Help and troubleshooting	Difficult to do over the phone or online	Easy – your bookkeeper or accountant logs in and both of you view the same information

Diagram 4.1 Traditional vs. Online accounting

The other benefits of using online accounting are:

- less administration hours and more time for business operations
- affordable monthly subscription plans
- mobile app available

With all these benefits that online accounting offers, you do not want to ignore them. There are a few online accounting systems in the market but the author mainly uses Xero. It is user-friendly and the functionalities are very intuitive for those who are used to Hotmail and Gmail. MYOB has also introduced their online versions *AccountRight Live* and *Live Accounts* which provide great benefits as well.

Xero as an online accounting software has only one version. It simplifies things and avoids confusion as to which version has what modules. For example, you can get your bank transactions fed into your Xero account and it matches probable entry based on past transactions. You save a lot of time keying in data from your documents to your accounting system. This is just one benefit of online accounting. To find out more, visit www.xero.com. You can try their free demo version for about a month. This will give you the opportunity to try if this is the software for you. Below is the Dashboard when you log into the demo company. The main accounts are shown here such as bank accounts, money coming in and going out, and also an account watch list. You can add and remove accounts in the watch list. There are also video guides that you can play on certain pages that show you how to set up things. Remember you are only using a demo version so take full advantage of it.

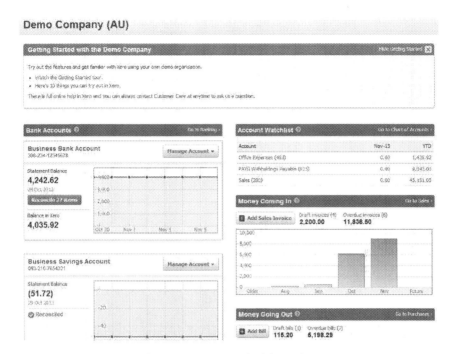

Diagram 4.2 Xero online accounting dashboard

When you set up your new company file in MYOB *AccountRight* (version 19.9), after putting your business information including the serial number of your MYOB software, it will ask about your accounting year. It will default to the current financial year you are in and automatically shows you the last month of the financial year. The 'Conversion Month' is the first month of the year. Continue and click next.

When you get to the part to build you accounts list, it may be easier if you start with the ones already provided by MYOB because you select the industry and the type of business.

Notes

Notes

Chapter 5

How to record income, expenses and other uncommon transactions

Capture from where transactions start

One of the best ways to capture information is from the point the amount of the transaction is established. This point may vary depending on the processes involved. For example, at your local food grocery shop, when the customer brings the products at the counter to pay, the recording process starts when the product barcode is scanned by an optical scanner. Once payment is received either through cash or card the transaction is settled. The method of payment may affect how fast the transaction is reflected on your accounting system. In Xero online accounting, if the customer pays by card (either debit or credit card) it does not take a while to feed that amount into the accounting system from your bank. They call it bank feeds as each line on the bank statement is fed into Xero. All you need to do when you log into your Xero account is to confirm those bank feeds. This process already saves you hours of data entry. This manual process is also prone to errors. With Xero, confirming all those transactions may take you 10-15 minutes. When customer pays in cash, that money is not deposited until the end of the day or the next day. Only when that happens that the bank feed is generated to be fed into Xero. If you want to start to avail of the great benefits of online accounting, jump onto www.xero.com and sign up so you can use the free DEMO version

The important thing about your BAS and being compliant is the processes you have in place. When you get audited about the figures declared on your BAS or income tax return, the individual entries on your accounting system is generally the first place to start. So it is very important that you have a good system in place. Remember that you also need to comply with the substantiation requirements and keep invoices for five years. Some invoices are printed on thermal paper and they fade after a few months. That is why it is recommended to scan invoices and save them on your computer. You can also use online storage websites such as Dropbox. You can start using Dropbox for free. Later, you can upgrade and start paying a nominal amount per month depending on your storage needs. Either way, as long as you have them saved somewhere safe and easily accessible so when you try to find an invoice during an audit you know exactly where to go.

There are five common issues that many small business owners have in recordkeeping:

1. <u>Whether to enter the amount of including or excluding GST</u>

   Most accounting packages can be set up with a default tax code when raising invoices. For example in Xero online accounting, there is an option at the top right whether the amount that you enter is Tax Exclusive, Tax Inclusive or No Tax. Depending on which option you pick, Xero will automatically calculate the GST and make the corresponding entry to the GST account without you having to manually enter the GST amount. This feature is similar to MYOB except that you either tick the invoice if it is tax-inclusive or leave it un-ticked if the amount is not tax-inclusive. This box is also located at the top right-hand side when you raise the invoice.

Diagram 5.1   Raising an invoice in Xero online accounting with options for Tax Exclusive, Tax Inclusive or No Tax codes. Xero then calculates and makes the entry automatically to the GST account

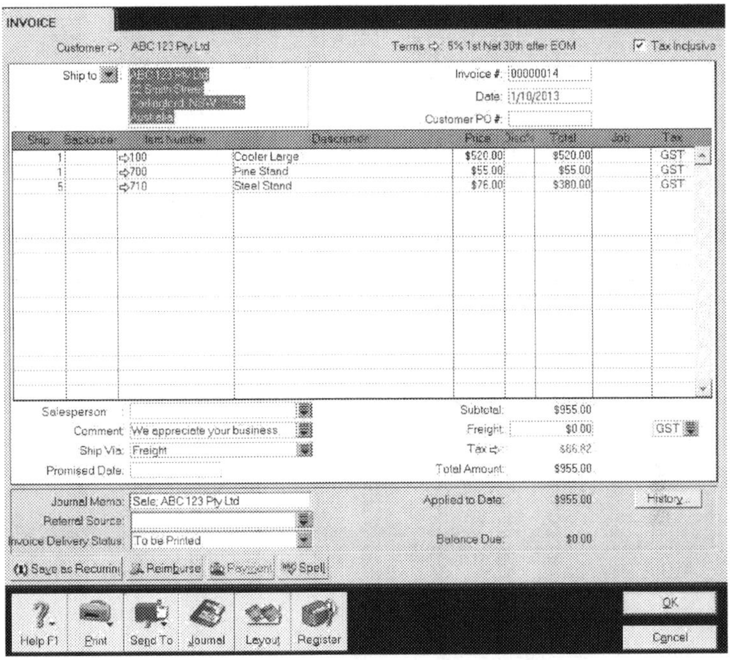

INVOICE								
Customer ⇨ ABC 123 Pty Ltd			Terms ⇨ 5% 1st Net 30th after EOM				☑ Tax Inclusive	

Ship to ▼ ABC 123 Pty Ltd
22 Smith Street
Gladesville NSW 2111

Invoice #: 00000014
Date: 1/10/2013
Customer PO #:

Ship	Backorder	Item Number	Description	Price	Disc%	Total	Job	Tax
1		⇨100	Cooler Large	$520.00		$520.00		GST
1		⇨700	Pine Stand	$55.00		$55.00		GST
5		⇨710	Steel Stand	$76.00		$380.00		GST

Salesperson:			Subtotal:	$955.00	
Comment:	We appreciate your business		Freight:	$0.00	GST ▼
Ship Via:	Freight		Tax ⇨:	$86.82	
Promised Date:			Total Amount:	$955.00	

Journal Memo:	Sale; ABC 123 Pty Ltd	Applied to Date:	$955.00	History...
Referral Source:				
Invoice Delivery Status:	To be Printed	Balance Due:	$0.00	

(X) Save as Recurring   Reimburse   Payment   Spell

Help F1   Print   Send To   Journal   Layout   Register

OK
Cancel

Diagram 5.2   **Raising an invoice in MYOB. You can either tick the Tax Inclusive box at the top right or leave it unticked. MYOB then calculates and automatically records the GST to the GST account**

2. Prepaid expenses

For small businesses (with turnover of less than $2 million), most prepaid expenses cover not more than 12 months which means they can be recorded as outright expenses. This is why the ATO introduced that 12-month rule for practicality and to make it easier for business owners as far as recordkeeping goes. The 12-month rule also states that the service period of the product or service ends in the income year following the year the income is incurred. If these conditions for the 12-month rule are not met, the prepayment needs to be apportioned over the period of service to a maximum of 10 years for amounts over $1,000. So for example you paid $20,000 on 1st October

2012 for your business rent for the period 1st December to 31 October 2013. The service period is ten months – the 12-month rule is satisfied. It starts in the financial year 2013 (July 2012-June 2013) and ends in 2014 (July 2013-June 2014).

3. Credit card repayments of expenses

When customers pay you by credit card the sale will be shown on your bank statement as a credit. Receiving credit card payment is not an issue, whether you are using Xero online accounting or MYOB. When you start paying by credit card that is when you need to keep track of your purchases made with that credit card and the payments you will make. The issue is generally when you make payments of any amount not taking into account the amounts of the individual purchases made with that credit card. To be more efficient and to save some time reconciling your credit card statements every month the total of your payments need to match the total of the individual purchases. For example, the following were paid through a credit card:

Diagram 5.3 Sample credit card statement entries

BAL BROUGHT FORWARD		134.60
Sept 8	CALTX	45.50
Sept 14	COLES	56.70
Sept 21	OFFCWRKS	534.30
TOTAL CURRENT PURCHASES		636.50
TOTAL BALANCE		771.10

Assuming you are low in funds this month and also have other suppliers to be paid. You decided to only pay the minimum monthly repayment amount of $100. This is a common habit of small business owners that makes it difficult to reconcile at the end of the month. It is because it cannot be specified which invoice or expense you are paying the amount for. So in our example above, instead of paying $100, consider paying the $45.50 and $56.70 totalling $102.2 so come recording time, those two amounts CALTX and COLES will be recorded as paid and the only outstanding account from the current month is the OFFCWRKS.

4. Rent and lease arrangements

The recording of commercial rent you pay for your premises is straightforward. Whether it is Xero or MYOB, the amount paid to the landlord is the amount shown on your profit and loss as rent which becomes part of G11 (non-capital purchases) on your BAS.

When businesses purchase assets, they often enter into a hire-purchase agreement where they make periodic payments until the end of the term. This is an area of bookkeeping that many professionals make it more complex than it needs to be. They try to dissect its components when it can be very simple. For example if you buy a car, regardless of who funds it (own money, loan bank or finance agreement), it is a purchase of an asset as far as accounting is concerned. It is recorded as an asset. Now, the GST part is where the most confusion lies. Do you claim the GST outright at the commencement of the agreement or proportionately every regular payment? Since it is a purchase and asset is recorded, GST is also claimed when you set up the asset account in your books. For example, you bought a computer financed by a hire-purchase arrangement for $3,300 including GST of $300. There are 48 monthly repayments of $100 totalling $4,800 by the end of the term. The difference of $1,500 is the interest. At the commencement of the agreement, the Xero manual journal entry will look like the following.

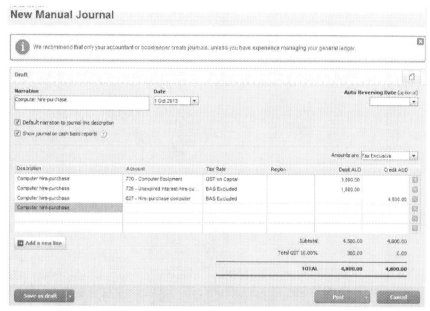

Diagram 5.4   **Manual journal in Xero to record the purchase of a computer by hire-purchase agreement**

Assuming direct debit is set up on your account for the repayment each month, it will be fed into your Xero account. Then you can separate the amounts that relate to interest and principal based on the amortisation schedule provided by the finance company. The amortisation schedule details the amount of repayment (including amounts that relate to interest and principal) throughout the life of the arrangement.

5. Private or domestic use

Oftentimes business funds are used to pay private expenses. This is common for small business owners to do but you need to ensure that this is properly accounted for. This is normally recorded by adding to the Drawings account. For example in Xero, when you use business money to pay for your son's university fees, the entry when you reconcile the bank feed will be:

Diagram 5.5 **Reconciling a bank feed that relates to private use of business funds**

Once the private use has been properly accounted for when they occur, you do not need to adjust G15 on your GST worksheet.

Separating the sales with GST from GST-free and input-taxed sales

The efficiency of your bookkeeping process depends largely on how you operate. Although we emphasise the benefits of online accounting, it may not be for everyone. You can still find ways to make your processes more efficient. You can use diagram 3.1 in Chapter 3 reproduced below as guide to think about possible improvements. For example if you are using a manual process, you can categorise transactions according to source (customers and suppliers; employees, owners and associates; government, bank and other entities).

(Reproduced from Chapter 3): Diagram 3.1 Process overview of the record-keeping and BAS compliance process

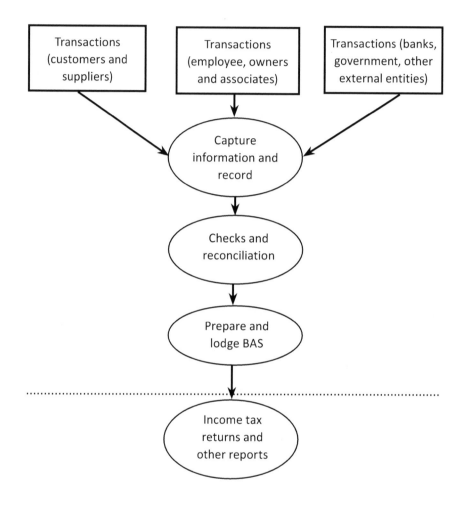

You can group all the documents (invoices, receipts, etc.) based on these categories and create a daily summary. Do this for all your sales and purchases. Do not put it off until the next day because next day becomes next week which becomes next month. By then you would have forgotten the details of the events surrounding the transactions and it would be very difficult and time-consuming to reconstruct them. This is particularly true for uncommon transactions. So make it a habit to at least summarise your daily sales and daily purchases. You may also want to sub-categorise them according to payment type such as cash, cheque and EFT. Then you will need to add up the total GST you collected from the sales and total GST you paid your suppliers. If you are in the food industry, print the list of food items that are GST-free as well as those that have GST and put them somewhere handy. Once you have done these steps, you would have the total amounts for the following:

Sales – GST (capital and non-capital)

Sales – GST-free

Sales – Input-taxed

Sales – Exports (if applicable)

Purchases – GST (capital and non-capital)

Purchases – GST-free

Purchases – Input-taxed

You can then record them into your accounting system. For MYOB users, the entries for sales and purchases would look like:

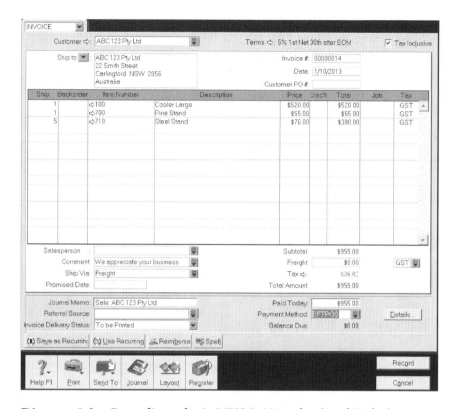

Diagram 5.6   **Recording sales in MYOB. Note that 'Paid Today' amount is the total of sales made for that day. By putting in that amount paid today, MYOB will automatically create an entry to record collection.**

Sales>Enter Sales

Just to summarise the steps in a manual process:

1. Categorise invoices and receipts according to entity source (suppliers or customers, employees, shareholders or directors, and bank, government or other entities)
2. Daily summarise all the normal sales and normal purchases
3. Calculate the amount of GST from your sales and from your purchases to include in your daily summary

4. For any uncommon transactions, identify whether the transaction involves money coming in or money coming out. When you receive money it can mainly either be (1) a sale of an asset or stock; or (2) a loan or investment to your business. It can also be as a result of a purchase return but we will not use that as an example.

<u>Sale of assets or stock</u>

An asset may be furniture, motor vehicle or any other business asset. Note that a disposal of an asset may result to what is called a balancing adjustment which is the difference between the termination value and the written down value. There are special rules on cost base and indexed cost based when assets are purchased before 21 September 1999. If the termination value (money received or to be received less disposal costs) from the sale is higher than the written down value (cost less accumulated depreciation), the general journal entry would look like:

Cash/Cheque	4,000	
Accumulated depreciation	3,000	
Asset		5,000
Gain on disposal		2,000

A sale of a stock will just be a normal daily entry to record sales (credit sales) and the payment received (debit cash or cheque) which is automatically created when you enter a sale in MYOB via *Sales*.

<u>Loans to or investments in your business</u>

Another possible source of money coming is if someone loans you money. This is recorded as a liability:

Cash/Cheque   5,000

Loan from John Boy   5,000

If it is an investment it will look like:

Cash/Cheque   5,000

Funds Introduced   5,000

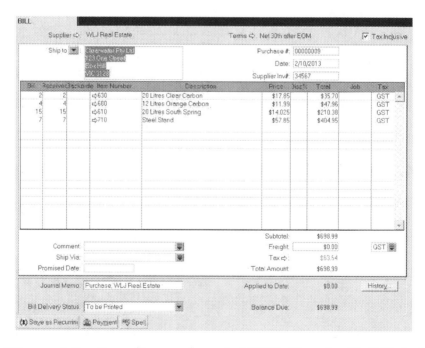

Diagram 5.7   **Recording purchases in MYOB. Note that 'Paid Today' amount zero as it is normal to buy stocks on account**

Purchases>Enter Purchases

When you pay the invoice as it falls due, you record the payment via *Purchases>Pay Bills*. Select the supplier and enter the amount being paid. Remember to make it a rule to always ask for a tax invoice so you do not need to worry about thresholds. For example, to be able to claim GST credits an invoice is required for purchases amounting to $75 excluding GST or $82.50 including GST.

Once in a while you may need to record uncommon transactions. One way to approach this is to identify whether the transaction is an *income/money coming in* transaction or *expense/money coming out*. Then establish whether GST is applicable. Bear in mind that when you use the *Sales* menu or *Purchases* menu, it will use the default cheque account. This means that the cheque account increases for every sale in the *Sales* menu and decreases for every purchase in the *Purchases* menu.

If you have employees you have to process them in the payroll system. There are quite a few important processes in payroll that you need to have an up-to-date system every year to comply with updated PAYG withholding tables, superannuation, child support deductions, salary sacrifice thresholds, garnishee deductions, among others. We are currently working on our second book on how to process payroll so subscribe to our mailing list on our website for updates.

In Xero online accounting, if all the sales and purchases are received and paid through your bank, those transactions (called bank feeds) will be fed into the bank transactions in Xero and all you have to do is confirm OK when you do your reconciliation. Since the bank feeds are updated daily, you can do your reconciliation daily and it will only take you a few minutes. That is why as much as possible always have transactions paid or received through your main business cheque account as opposed to cash so they appear on the bank statement that you can review later on.

Trading stock

There are simplified trading stock rules that you may be eligible to use. You can choose not to conduct a stocktake to account for the changes in the value of your stock if the difference of your stock at the end of the year from the beginning of the income year is $5,000 or less. You access this concession at the end of the year when you calculate amounts for your tax return.

There are currently three methods on how to value your stock:

1. Cost
2. Market selling value
3. Replacement value

Cost

This amount includes all amounts connected with bringing the stock into existence. Examples of costs that are included are purchase price, freight, customs duties and delivery charges. For manufactured goods and work in progress, they are the cost of labour and materials (full-cost) and proportion of the fixed and variable factory overhead. Examples of the variable factory overhead are rent, electricity and administration.

Market Selling Value

This is the current value of your stock you sell in your normal course of business.

Replacement value

This value is the amount of a substantially similar item if you replace it. This is normally the amount in the buying market on the last day of the financial or income year.

Notes

Notes

Chapter 6

GST – what to watch out for

GST overview

GST is a consumption tax. The rate is 10% and is levied on most goods and services sold and consumed in Australia. Although you pay GST on the taxable supplies you sell you also claim input tax credits for your purchases.

If you are a food retailer, you may need to download Simplified GST accounting methods for food retailers (NAT 3185) from www.ato.gov.au or just google NAT 3185. It explains the Snapshot GST Accounting Method (SAM). This is one of five simplified GST accounting methods you can use. The other four are:

- Business norms
- Stock purchases
- Sales percentage
- Purchases snapshot

With Business norms method, your business needs to be one listed by the ATO that has standard percentages determined by the ATO. This means that you do not need to work out how much GST sales or GST-free sales you have made for a tax period. All you need to do is apply the percentage provided by the ATO. You will need to satisfy other conditions such having a turnover of $2 million or less and not having adequate point-of-sale equipment.

Type of retail business	GST-free sales	GST-free purchases of stock
Cake shops	2%	95%
Hot bread shops	50%	75%
Rural convenience stores	Converters: 22.5% Non-converters: 30%	30% 30%
Continental delicatessens	85%	90%
Convenience stores that prepare takeaway food but do not sell fuel or alcohol	22.5%	30%
Convenience stores that do not prepare takeaway food and do not sell fuel or alcohol	30%	30%
Fresh fish retailers	35%	98%
Health food shops	35%	35%
Pharmacies that also sell food	Dispensary:non-claimable 98% Over the counter: 47.5%	NIL 2%

A few notes about GST if you are in the food industry:

- You cannot claim GST credits for food used as entertainment expense if you cannot claim an income tax deduction for it
- You must charge GST to customers and pay to the ATO is food and drinks are sold and consumed at a restaurant,

café, snack bar, theatre, amusement park, cinema, gallery, gym or a sports ground

If you use MYOB *AccountRight*, when you enter the transactions you need to use separate accounts for those that have GST from those that do not have GST. For those who use a standard cash register which is not linked to your accounting system, ensure that you print your daily sales summary from your cash register. If you have not done this before or not sure how to do this, please refer to the manual or ring the help line of the cash register company you bought it from. You can also google the model and brand of your cash register and you may be able to find something online. Once you have your sales summary, you can then record the GST sales and GST free sales in MYOB. An example of how a sales receipt might look like is shown below. Please note that different brands of cash registers may produce different receipt formats.

```
.................................................................

DAILY

FOOD      QT        35
                    $103.70

BOX       QT        1
                    $10

ITEMS     QT        3
                    $17.20

.................................................................

GROSS TOTAL QT          39
                        $130.90
```

NET TOTAL   8

$128.10

TAXABLE AMOUNT $103.37

GST AMOUNT $10.33

=====================================

Diagram 6.1 Sample cash register receipt

Using the sample receipt above for a grocery shop, we can see that the sale amount with GST included is $103.37 which is labelled as TAXABLE AMOUNT. The GST is not included in this amount. We need to add GST on top of that. The GST rate of 10% multiplied by the TAXABLE AMOUNT of $103.37 is $10.33 which is shown on a separate line called GST. We can also see on the receipt that other sales without the GST amounted to $17.20. We assume that this is GST-free because the sale with GST is already shown separately. The total GST sale of $103.37 plus $10.33 and the GST-free sale to $17.20 total $130.90. When entering the sales in MYOB, ensure that you use the correct module. If you are recording a cash sale that was not previously recorded you can use the 'Banking' module then 'Receive Money.' Ensure that when you enter the sales amount inclusive of GST that the 'Tax Inclusive' box is ticked at the top right hand side. By ticking that, MYOB will work out the GST amount and will post it to the GST account.

A payment for a previously recorded sale in the 'Sales' menu, is also entered via the 'Sales' menu in 'Receive Payment' by selecting the invoice to which the payment relates to. Now, this is where some issues may arise because some customers pay by instalments and their calculation may not be the same as yours. It is very important to communicate with your clients and ensure that you have the same calculation including the breakdown of the invoices included in the instalment plan.

Your daily sales summary will have the total of these amounts at the end of the day so ensure to print this out at the end of day and scan or take a photo using your smart phone and save on your computer. Create folders for every month on your computer and then subfolders for each type of expense or account. This way when you want to reconcile figures at the end of the month or year, you can easily find them. The subfolders arrangement would look like:

2013

    July

        Office supplies

        Cleaning

        Council rates

    August

        Office supplies

        Cleaning

        Council rates

GST in Xero online accounting

In Xero online accounting, there is a separate account called GST where both GST paid and GST collected are recorded. It is shown under the currently liabilities section of the Balance Sheet. If the GST collected from customers is more than the GST paid to suppliers, it will have positive balance in the current liability section. If however, the GST paid is more than the GST collected, it will have a negative balance indicated by parentheses.

Liabilities

Current Liabilities	
Accounts Payable	8,507.78
GST	1,188.88
Historical Adjustment	19,212.21
Owner A Funds Introduced	550.00
PAYG Withholdings Payable	9,042.00
Total Current Liabilities	**38,500.87**

Diagram 6.2 GST collected from customers is more than GST paid to suppliers

Liabilities

Current Liabilities	
Accounts Payable	8,507.78
GST	(511.12)
Historical Adjustment	19,212.21
Owner A Funds Introduced	550.00
PAYG Withholdings Payable	9,042.00
Total Current Liabilities	**36,800.87**
Total Liabilities	**36,800.87**

Diagram 6.3 GST paid to suppliers is more than GST collected from customers

Common GST errors

Below is a list of the common GST errors that you need to watch out for, in addition to the ones illustrated previously. It is recommended to familiarise yourself with these items so you know what to watch out for when you start the process of capturing, recording and preparing your BAS.

Diagram 6.4 Common GST errors

Commons GST and BAS errors	Ways to minimise if not eliminate errors
Transposition of figures	Implement online accounting where bank transactions are fed into your accounting system automatically and therefore there is no need for manual entry
Incorrect application of discounts	Use a checklist to check discounts regularly – it increases the GST credit for your purchases and decreases your GST liability from your sales
Incorrect setup accounts	Use account description which closely matches ATO's description in its list of GST, GST free and input-taxed items and set up tax codes accordingly
Incorrect use of tax codes	Take time to establish which sales accounts you are going to use frequently for each customer and try to set up an account just for that supplier
Not reconciling bank statements with records	Implement online accounting where bank transactions are fed into your accounting system automatically and therefore reconciliation is kept at minimum
No stock-take records	Set up reminders starting from April to take inventory on 30th of June every year

Not withholding 46.5% from suppliers without ABN for amounts $75 excluding GST	Make it a rule to ask for a proper tax invoice with ABN regardless of amount so you do not even have to worry about withholding 46.5%
Not issuing proper tax invoices for sales and not keeping tax invoices for purchases	Make it a rule to issue tax invoice regardless of amount and always ask for tax invoices for all your purchases
Wages and superannuation included in G11	Ensure Wages and Superannuation accounts have tax code of N-T and set up in *BASlink*. Only wages and other payments from which amounts were withheld are included in W1. For the full list see Chapter 10
Not keeping log book to substantiate motor vehicle claims	Ensure that you maintain a log book for your trips noting which ones are business kilometres. There are four methods to claim motor vehicle expenses (including the log book method) and you can choose whichever gives the highest claim. Keep motor vehicle relates receipts
Putting NIL or N/A instead of the number 0 or leaving it blank	If there are no amounts to be reported put zeros at G1, 1A, 1B, 5A, 9 and T1 if applicable and leave blank at G2, W1, W2, W3, W4 and W5 if applicable
Unsure whether to leave blank or the number zero	If there are no amounts to be reported put zeros at G1, 1A, 1B, 5A, 9 and T1 if applicable and leave blank at G2, W1, W2, W3, W4 and W5 if applicable

Incorrect use of the GST accounting method	If you are using cash method sales and purchases are recorded based on how much was paid or received regardless of the invoice amount. Accrual method is recording the transaction the earlier of when payment or invoice is received for sales and the earlier of when the invoice is paid or invoice issued
Changing the reason for PAYG instalment and not using the correct reason code	See list in Chapter 10
Lodging photocopied statements instead of original	Ensure only original BAS documents are lodged with the ATO
Not registering with the Tax Office for tax obligations reported in your activity statement	It is important to ensure that you are correctly registered for all your tax obligations. To register or cancel registration for PAYG withholding, GST, luxury car tax (LCT) or wine equalisation tax (WET) ring the ATO on **13 28 66**
Not including cash taken from the cash register or till used to pay for purchases	Total sales (G1 on your BAS) should include all cash payments made out of the till for purchases because those cash payments came from your cash sales

| Not lodging your BAS by the due date | If you are a small business owner set a reminder up a month before the due date. A month is a reasonable time not too soon that you may not have enough time and not too early that you tend to ignore

The only time you do not have to lodge is if you receive an instalment notice in which they indicate the letter N, R, S or T in the top left-hand corner. When you receive this notice pay the pre-printed instalment amount by the due date |
| Some labels or boxes such as 1A (GST sales or GST instalment) and 5A (PAYG income tax instalment) are often overlooked | Always review your BAS after completing it to ensure you have not missed anything

You must complete 1A if you are reporting a GST obligation and 5A if you are reporting a PAYG obligation (even when your instalment amount is zero) |

Not all amounts are being correctly reported at G1	You should include all payments and other consideration you have received during the quarter for sales you have made in the course of your business. This includes amounts you have shown at G2 (Export sales), G3 (GST-free) and input taxed supplies like interest on investments and rent on residential properties (shown at G4 if you are using the calculation sheet method). The following amounts should not be reported at G1: <ul><li>inter-entity loans</li><li>transfers between bank accounts</li><li>private money</li><li>other entities' income (e.g. rent for rental property that is in another entity's name/ individual's name)</li></ul>
Completing other boxes relating to other options for GST obligations other than the option you have choses	Complete the boxes for one option only
G2 (Export sales) is completed incorrectly (e.g. treating supplies as exports when the goods are consumed within Australia)	You should report the following only at G2: <ul><li>the free on board value of exported goods that meet the GST-free export rules</li><li>payments for the repairs of goods from overseas that are to be exported, and</li><li>Payments for goods used in the repair of goods from overseas that are to be exported</li></ul>

Claiming GST credits on the total price of a car that exceeds the luxury car threshold amount ($60,316 for the FY 2013–14 for non-fuel efficient cars and $75,375 for fuel-efficient cars)	GST credits for cars with a GST-inclusive price that exceeds the threshold value are restricted to a maximum of 1/11th of that value ($60,316 for the FY 2013–14 for non-fuel efficient cars and $75,375 for fuel-efficient cars)
Claiming GST credits: • for bank fees and charges, third party insurance and stamp duty • for the full amount of a purchase, even when the goods are to be used partially • for private purposes, or • where the supplier of the goods or services is not registered for GST	• You cannot claim for bank fees and charges, third party insurance and stamp duty • You can only claim for the business portion of the expense • You cannot claim if the supplier is not registered for GST. You must also hold a valid tax invoice when you make your claim • You must also hold a valid tax invoice when you make your claim
Not including the sale of a business	The sale price of a business, including any GST, must be reported at G1 Where the sale is a GST-free sale of a going concern, you also include this amount at G3 Where the sale is taxable, you must report the GST amount at 1A
Not providing your estimated net GST for the year when requesting a variation to your GST instalment amount	When varying GST instalments, an estimated annual net GST amount must be provided in G22

Notifying a variation to your GST or PAYG Instalment after the due date for the instalment to be paid	The law requires you to notify the Tax Office of your variations by the date the instalment is due to be paid
Claiming GST credits for the full amount of a purchase, even when the goods are to be used partially for private purposes	You can only claim GST credits on the proportion of the expense used for business
GST adjustment and the income tax effect. You were unaware that you are subject to an increasing adjustment at G1 on your previous activity statement for assets disposed of	GST needs to be accounted for on an asset disposal. You may not have identified a GST amount and included the GST inclusive value on your tax return. If you sell a business asset you will generally need to account for GST and include the price of the asset sold at G1 and the GST payable at 1A on your activity statement. When completing your income tax return you need to ensure that the GST exclusive amount of the asset is included in business income. All income amounts included on the return should be exclusive of GST. Including the GST inclusive amount of the asset will overstate your business income and you will pay additional income tax
Claiming GST credits where the contractor or supplier is not registered or required to be registered for GST	You cannot claim GST credits where the contractor or supplier of the goods or services is not registered or required to be registered for GST as no GST is included in the price

Changing the legal structure of your business entity and continuing to lodge activity statements under the ABN of the old entity	If you change the legal structure of the entity used to carry on your business, you cannot continue lodging your activity statements under the same ABN. You need to apply for a new ABN and register the new entity for GST if that entity is required to be registered for GST, or chooses to register for GST Examples of changes in legal structure includes: • changing from a sole trader to a partnership, trust or company, or vice-versa, and • reconstituting a partnership
Not explaining the variations or not providing a variation code	When you vary a GST or PAYG instalment amount, you must also say why you made the variation at label G24 (for GST) or label T4 (for PAYG)
Claiming full GST credits on the purchase of real property (or deposit for same) at the time of entering into a standard land contract	If you hold a tax invoice, you claim the GST credit for the deposit or full payment of a creditable purchase of land under a completed standard land contract in the activity statement for the tax period in which settlement occurs. This applies whether or not you account for GST on a cash basis

You have shown total sales at G1 but left 1A and/or G3 blank	If you have selected GST option 1 or 2 and your total sales amount at G1 is more than zero, you must show an amount for GST on sales at 1A and other GST-free sales at G3 If you have nothing to report at 1A and/or G3, show zero at these labels
No reason code is shown if varying your instalment	If you vary your PAYG instalment amount or rate, or your GST amount, you must show one of the following reason codes at label T4 (for PAYG instalments) or label G24 (for GST) on your activity statement Visit *How to vary quarterly PAYG instalments* or phone **13 28 66** The reason codes are in *Chapter 10 How to prepare and lodge your BAS using accounting software*
GST credits are claimed without a tax invoice	You must have a valid tax invoice to GST credits
When accounting for GST on a cash basis, GST credits are claimed at the commencement of a hire purchase or lease contract	GST credits may only be claimed at the time a repayment is made for a hire purchase or lease contract, when accounting for GST on a cash basis
Claiming GST credits for the full amount of a purchase, even when the goods or services are used partially for private purposes	GST credits may only be claimed for the business portion of the expense

Including private expenses when claiming GST credits and deductions on business income tax returns	Private expenses should not be included on your activity statements or income tax returns. This means if you have one bank account for both your business and private purposes, you need to separate the amounts
When reporting PAYG tax withheld the amount at W5 (total of amounts withheld) often incorrectly includes the amount at W1 (total salary, wages and other payments)	If you are required to report PAYG tax withheld, only add amounts at: • W2 (amount withheld from total salary wages and other payments) • W3 (other amounts withheld), and • W4 (amount withheld where no ABN quoted) to calculate W5 (total of amounts withheld)
You completed label 4, or one of the W labels, even though you are not registered for PAYG withholding	If you pay salary and wages and you are not registered for PAYG withholding, phone 13 28 66
Reporting total salary, wages and other payments (W1), but not reporting amounts withheld from these payments (W2)	Amounts withheld from salary, wages and other payments must be reported at W2 (unless you are a Large PAYG remitter)
Not reporting amounts withheld from payments when an ABN has not been quoted (W4)	Where an ABN has not been quoted, amounts withheld from payments must be reported at label W4

Incorrect recording of instalment income at T1	You must include all your earnings in your instalment income. This includes amounts that are paid by direct credit to your bank account and all cash (even if it has not been banked or was used to pay expenses). You must also account for your non-cash transactions (e.g. those resulting from bartering) in your instalment income
Not providing your estimated tax for the year when requesting a variation to your PAYG instalment amount	If you use Option 1 and vary your PAYG instalment for the quarter, please ensure you complete T8 and T9. The Tax Office uses your estimated tax at T8 to work out your instalments for the remaining quarters of the income year
There is PAYG instalment obligation but haven't calculated the amount at 5A correctly	Your PAYG instalment amount at 5A must equal: • T1 x T2 (PAYG instalment income) x (PAYG instalment rate) or • T1 x T3 (PAYG instalment income) x (varied PAYG instalment rate), or • T7 (Pre-printed instalment amount), or • T9 (Varied instalment amount)
Reporting net income at Label T1	Total gross income (excluding GST) is reported at label T1

Not reporting instalment income at label T1 but reporting total sales at label G1	Generally, the presence of sales for GST purposes means that there must be at least that amount of instalment income reported at T1. Instalment income reported at T1 also includes other income such as dividends and interest
Not reporting instalment income at label T1 when T1 is zero	T1 must be completed if it is zero when the Commissioner rate (T2) is used for reporting instalment income
Adjusting T1 figure to reflect a change in expected tax liability	Commissioner rate (T2) should be varied using T3 to reflect a change in expected tax liability
Individuals lodging a quarterly PAYG I activity statement are not including their income from partnerships and trusts as instalment income at label T1 on a quarterly basis	Individuals who lodge a quarterly PAYG I activity statement must include their share of income from partnerships and trusts as instalment income at label T1 each quarter
Lodging activity statements after your FBT return	If you pay fringe benefits tax (FBT) by instalments, make sure you lodge all your activity statements for the FBT year ending 31 March before you lodge your FBT return. This includes the March quarter activity statement due on 28 April. This will allow the ATO to update your FBT account and process your return quickly

Not including FBT on private use of business assets (especially for cars and computers	FBT obligations for private use of business assets must be reported in your FBT return
Claiming GST input tax credits on the full amount of the meal entertainment benefits	Only claim input tax credits on benefits that you pay FBT on, e.g. using the 50/50 method you only claim 50% of the total input tax credits

Notes

Notes

Chapter 7

How to record and reconcile salaries and wages, PAYG withholding, PAYG instalment

<u>Payroll checklist</u>

When you have two employees you may think paying them is an easy process, but if you start going through the payroll compliance checklist you will realise that is not an easy task. There are minimum mandatory requirements involved that relate to employees and there are hefty penalties for non-compliance. It is recommended to use an accounting system that has payroll capabilities that can accurately calculate PAYG withholding, superannuation, salary sacrifice (if applicable), deductions such as child support, leave entitlements (annual, personal, long service) and also generate payslips every payday and payments summaries at the end of the financial year. You also need to determine your employees are covered by industry awards or individual agreements. Large businesses have additional payroll requirements such as payroll tax when they reach a certain gross payments threshold. To summarise the basic minimum payroll requirements, below is a list of the basic things that you need to establish when paying employees:

1. Award or individual agreements
2. PAYG withholding

3. Superannuation
4. Salary sacrifice (if applicable)
5. Deductions such as child support (if applicable)
6. Leave entitlements (annual, personal, long service, etc.)
7. Payroll tax (state tax that is generally for businesses that reach a certain gross payments threshold per state)

If you are unsure about anything you can ring Fair Work on 13 13 94 or visit their website www.fairwork.gov.au.

Tax tables

Depending on how often you pay your employees you need to withhold tax from the salaries and wages you pay your employees. This is called PAYG withholding and you need to check with the ATO if you are registered. Generally you apply for PAYG withholding at the same time you apply for an ABN using the same form. If you are not yet registered but you have an ABN, you can apply online on www.abr.gov.au or through your business portal https://bp.ato.gov.au. Please also refer to Chapter 3 under the topic PAYG withholding.

There are tax tables from www.ato.gov.au that you can download to calculate the PAYG tax to be withheld from the employees. If you use the traditional MYOB software, you will receive a CD towards the end of the financial year to let you know of any updates you need which may include changes in PAYG withholding amounts.

How PAYG is calculated, reported and paid

To show you how PAYG withholding is calculated let's say you employ someone called Joey Smith. You pay him every week. Therefore you will need the weekly PAYG withholding tax table.

Below is an excerpt (page 3) of the 2013 weekly tax table from www.ato.gov.au that we will use in our example.

Diagram 7.1   Page 3 excerpt of the weekly PAYG withholding tax table from www.ato.gov.au

WEEKLY TAX TABLE – INCORPORATING MEDICARE LEVY

	Amount to be withheld	
Weekly earnings	With tax-free threshold	No tax-free threshold
1	2	3
$	$	$
426.00	17.00	101.00
427.00	17.00	101.00
428.00	17.00	102.00
429.00	18.00	102.00
430.00	18.00	102.00
431.00	18.00	103.00
432.00	19.00	103.00
433.00	19.00	104.00
434.00	19.00	104.00
435.00	19.00	104.00
436.00	20.00	105.00
437.00	20.00	105.00
438.00	20.00	105.00
439.00	21.00	106.00
440.00	21.00	106.00
441.00	21.00	106.00
442.00	21.00	107.00
443.00	22.00	107.00
444.00	22.00	107.00
445.00	22.00	108.00
446.00	23.00	108.00
447.00	23.00	108.00
448.00	23.00	109.00

449.00	24.00	109.00
450.00	24.00	109.00
451.00	24.00	110.00
452.00	24.00	110.00
453.00	25.00	110.00
454.00	25.00	111.00
455.00	25.00	111.00
456.00	26.00	111.00
457.00	26.00	112.00
458.00	26.00	112.00
459.00	26.00	112.00
460.00	27.00	113.00
461.00	27.00	113.00
462.00	27.00	113.00
463.00	28.00	114.00
464.00	28.00	114.00
465.00	28.00	114.00
466.00	28.00	115.00
467.00	28.00	115.00
468.00	29.00	116.00
469.00	29.00	116.00
470.00	29.00	116.00
471.00	29.00	117.00
472.00	29.00	117.00
473.00	30.00	117.00
474.00	30.00	118.00
475.00	30.00	118.00
476.00	30.00	118.00
477.00	31.00	119.00
478.00	31.00	119.00
479.00	31.00	119.00
480.00	31.00	120.00
481.00	31.00	120.00
482.00	32.00	120.00
483.00	32.00	121.00
484.00	32.00	121.00
485.00	32.00	121.00

486.00	32.00	122.00
487.00	33.00	122.00
488.00	33.00	122.00
489.00	33.00	123.00
490.00	33.00	123.00
491.00	33.00	123.00
492.00	34.00	124.00
493.00	34.00	124.00
494.00	34.00	124.00
495.00	34.00	125.00
496.00	34.00	125.00
497.00	35.00	125.00
498.00	35.00	126.00
499.00	35.00	126.00
500.00	35.00	126.00
501.00	35.00	127.00
502.00	36.00	127.00
503.00	36.00	128.00
504.00	36.00	128.00
505.00	36.00	128.00
506.00	36.00	129.00
507.00	37.00	129.00
508.00	37.00	129.00
509.00	37.00	130.00
510.00	37.00	130.00

Assume you are the owner and the employer of Joey Smith and you pay him $470 per week. If you look up the earnings on the first column, you will get the amount of tax to be withheld across on the second column if the employee claims tax-free threshold or third column if the employee does not claim the tax-free threshold. Assume that when Joey started he indicated on his Tax File Number (TFN) declaration form to claim the tax-free threshold. Therefore, in our example we will use the second column amount of tax to be withheld which is $29. The amount you pay Joey will be $441 which is the gross of $470 less tax of $29.

The general journal entry to record weekly payment:

Debit: **Wages** 470

Credit: **PAYG withholding** 29

Credit: **Cheque account** 441

When you remit the PAYG withheld to the ATO when you lodge your BAS, the entry will be:

Debit: **PAYG withholding** 29

Credit: **Cheque account** 29

Let us modify our example and assume that you paid Joey four times a month for three months (quarter). Total gross payments will be $470 x 4 x 3 = $5,640; Total PAYG withheld will be $348; and total net payments will be $5,292. When you make the weekly payments your entry would be the first entry above. When you prepare you BAS at the end of the quarter and remit the total PAYG withheld to the ATO, the entry will be:

Debit: **PAYG withholding** 348

Credit: **Cheque account** 348

The total amount you show under label **W2** will then be $348 and the total wages on **W1** will be $5640.

PAYG instalment

Pay As You Go (PAYG) instalment system is an instalment for expected income tax liability. The income can either be from business or investments. At the end of the year when your income is assessed, the amount you have paid to date will be credited to your tax liability to work out if there's a refund or more tax owing. The ATO uses your previous tax return to estimate tax liability. Generally those who earn $2000 or more will be notified of the instalment unless the latest notice of assessment is less than $500; or if the notional tax is less than $250; or if you are entitled to a senior's or pensioner's tax offset. Companies get notified if their instalment rate is more than 0%; or if notional tax is more than $250. Those companies that have $2 million in business and investment income pay using the instalment rate option.

When the ATO calculates the estimate tax liability it takes into account the likely growth in your business and investment income based on the GDP. The ATO will advise you how often you will make the payments on your BAS.

Generally, all you need to do with PAYG instalment is pay what the ATO tells you to pay at label **T7**.

W4 is the label on your BAS for amounts withheld where no ABN is quoted. If there are no withheld amounts this label is left blank. **W3** is for other amounts withheld (excluding any amount shown at W2 or W4) for example interest, dividends or royalty payments you made to a non-resident; payments made to a non-resident (interest, dividends, royalty) where the person has not completed a Tax File Number declaration form (form code is NAT3092); payments made to foreign residents for sports, entertainment, casino gaming junket activities and construction; DASP (departing Australia superannuation payments). These two labels (W4 and W3) are not often used so do not get these confused with **W1** and **W2**.

Fair Work on minimum wage

The 2013 national minimum wage for adults per week is $622.20 or $16.37 per hour. Casuals covered by the national minimum wage is $20.30 which is 24% extra than the full-time rate. You can find the award applicable to your employees on http://www. fairwork.gov.au/pay/finding-the-right-pay/pages/default.aspx.

In 2013, Fair Work released updates on the national wages. The national minimum wages for apprentices and juniors who do not have an award or agreement from the 1ˢᵗ of July 2013 are the following.

Diagram 7.2 National minimum wages - Apprentices

Year of apprenticeship	% of the level 3 adult hourly rate ($19.07)	Minimum hourly rate
1	55%	$10.49
2	65%	$12.39
3	80%	$15.25
4	95%	$18.11

Diagram 7.2 National minimum wages - Juniors

Age	% of national minimum wage	Minimum hourly rate
Under 16	36.8%	$6.03
16	47.3%	$7.74
17	57.8%	$9.46
18	68.3%	$11.18
19	82.5%	$13.51
20	97.7%	$16.00

Employees vs contractors

Another issue that Fair Work and the Australian Taxation Office are constantly facing is if workers are employees or contractors. You need to look at the whole arrangement to determine if the worker is employee or contractor. A worker is not a contractor just because he or she has an ABN. There are obligations for employers such as PAYG withholding, superannuation, among others relating to employees that is why you need to be careful and not just consider workers as contractors.

The difference between an employee and a contractor is that the former works in your business whereas a contractor is running his or her own business.

The Australian Taxation Office provided an outline of some of the differences based on six factors.

Diagram 7.3 Differences between employees and contractors based on six categories

	Employee	Contractor
Equipment, tools and other assets	your business provides all or most of the equipment, tools and other assets required to complete the work, or	the worker provides all or most of the equipment, tools and other assets required to complete the work
	the worker provides all or most of the equipment, tools and other assets required to complete the work, but your business provides them with an allowance or reimburses them for the cost of the equipment, tools and other assets.	the worker does not receive an allowance or reimbursement for the cost of this equipment, tools and other assets.
Basis of payment	the worker is paid for the time worked a price per item or activity a commission.	the worker is paid for a result achieved based on the quote they provided.
Ability to sub-contract/ delegate	the worker cannot sub-contract/delegate the work - they cannot pay someone else to do the work.	the worker is free to sub-contract/delegate the work - they can pay someone else to do the work.
Control over the work	your business has the right to direct the way in which the worker performs their work.	the worker has freedom in the way the work is done subject to the specific terms in any contract or agreement.

Independence	the worker is not operating independently from your business. They work within and are considered part of your business.	the worker is operating their own business independently from your business. The worker performs services as specified in their contract or agreement and is free to accept or refuse additional work.
Commercial risks	the worker takes no commercial risks. Your business is legally responsible for the work performed by the worker and liable for the cost of rectifying any defect in the work.	the worker takes commercial risks, with the worker being legally responsible for their work and liable for the cost of rectifying any defect in their work.

End of year

At the end of the financial year you issue payment summaries (individual non-business) to your employees. A payment summary mainly shows the gross payments including any allowances made to the employees, PAYG tax withheld, deductions such as union fees, salary sacrifice which is classified as Reportable Employer Superannuation Contribution (RESC), Reportable Fringe Benefits (RFB) if any and workplace giving.

The total of all the wages declared at label **W1** for the four quarters should be the total of the gross payments of all payment summaries.

Notes

Notes

Chapter 8

How to record depreciation and motor vehicle expenses

Uniform Capital Allowance (UCA)

Decline in value which is commonly known as depreciation is governed by Uniform Capital Allowance (UCA) rules from 1st of July 2001. For certain tangible assets that cost $100 or less, you get an immediate deduction for the cost to the extent that you used it for a taxable purpose. There is also the optional low-value pool arrangement for those depreciating assets with a cost or opening adjustable value of less than $1,000. The **low-cost** asset is a depreciating asset that has a cost of less than $1,000 after adjustments or GST credits. The **low-value** asset is a depreciating asset that has an opening adjustable value of less than $1,000. The adjustable value is the amount after decline in value has been deducted using the diminishing value method. These low-cost and low-value depreciating assets are allocated to a low-value pool and depreciated at statutory rates (generally 37.5% and 18.75% for newly acquired assets).

There are transitional rules for assets acquired before 1st of July 2001. If you do own these assets check form NAT 1996 from www.ato.gov.au for the special rules.

Methods of calculating decline in value

There are generally two methods to work out the decline in value of depreciating assets and once you have chosen a method for a particular asset you cannot change to the other method for that asset.

1. Prime cost
2. Diminishing value

There are cases however when only one method is available. For example, intangible assets such as in-house software, spectrum licenses, datacasting transmitted licenses and telecommunications access rights are depreciated using the prime cost method.

Assets that have been allocated to a low-value pool or software development tool are depreciated at a calculated statutory rate.

The prime cost assumes that the value of the depreciating asset decreases uniformly over its useful life. The formula depreciating using the prime cost method is:

Base value x **days held/365** x **100%/asset's effective life**

The diminishing value method assumes that the decline in value of a depreciating asset each year is a constant proportion of the remaining value and produces a progressively smaller over time. The formula for the diminishing value method is:

Base value x **days held/365** x **200%/asset's effective life**

This formula is for depreciating assets you started to hold on or after 10 May 2006. The base value is the cost of the asset or the opening adjustable value (plus any second element costs that income year). Second element cost is the amount paid after the time the asset is brought to its present location. The first element is the amount you pay for hold or acquire the asset.

Generally you have the choice of either using the effective life of a depreciating asset determined by the Commissioner or working it out yourself. If you are a small business owner it is recommended to use the Commissioner's determination. The Commissioner takes into account the general industry circumstances of an asset's use.

Simplified depreciation rules for small business entity

You are eligible to use the small business entities rules if you are a small business entity. You are a small business entity if your turnover in the current or previous financial year is less than $2 million. Once you are eligible you can avail of the following starting from financial year 2013.

- Depreciating assets with cost of less than $6,500 each can be written off immediately
- Other depreciating assets are pooled in a general small business pool with a depreciation rate of 30% or 15% in the first year

Once you choose to stop using the simplified depreciation concession, you cannot choose it again until at least five years after that financial or income year in which you opted to stop. If you currently use the simplified depreciation concession and considering cancelling it you need to think about the benefits of having simplified calculations and record-keeping that you will forgo. Think it through.

Note that these rules apply to the taxable purpose proportion which is basically the reasonable estimate of the extent you will use or have installed ready for use a depreciating asset for a taxable purpose.

Motor vehicle

There are five things you need to know about recording relating to motor vehicles:

1. Acquisition
2. During the life (depreciation)
3. Disposal
4. Substantiation methods
5. Private use portion

Acquisition and disposal

Motor vehicle for GST purposes means motor-powered road vehicle designed to carry a load of less than one tonne and less than nine passengers. It does not include motorcycle or similar vehicle. It also does not include graders, tractors and earthmoving equipment which you may want to record as Other Assets instead of Motor Vehicle. When you purchase a motor vehicle, the amount you paid is shown separately on the BAS at label G10 and claim the GST credit if you are registered for GST and use it to carry on your business. The GST credit is included at label 1B. Do not worry about the BAS labels. This is detailed in Chapter 10. Note that the amount shown on the BAS is only the business portion subject to a car limit. For the financial year 2013-14, the limit is $57,466. This means that the maximum amount you can claim at G10 is $57,466 and the GST credit is $5224 (1/11 x $57,466). Note that this is different from the Luxury car tax threshold of $60,316 in the 2013-14 financial year for LCT purposes. There are certain circumstances that the full amount of GST credit can be included. Under these examples, the vehicle must be used solely in carrying on your business. Examples are when:

1. You hold the car as a trading stock
2. It is an emergency vehicle
3. You export the car where the export is GST-free
4. The principal purpose is not designed to carry passengers
5. It is a vehicle specifically fitted out for transporting disabled people in wheelchairs

Other instances where you can claim GST credits are when you buy a second-hand car from someone who is not registered for GST but your intention was to sell it. When you sell the car for more than $300, you can claim the GST credit. However, you need to choose the lesser of:

- One-eleventh of the amount you paid for the car; or
- The amount of the GST payable when you sell the car

When you sell or dispose of the car do not forget to include the sale value or market value or trade-in value at **G1** and the related GST at **1A**.

There are also special rules for charity institutions and government schools and vehicles used to make financial suppliers or for private purpose. The disposal of motor vehicle by a charitable institution for example will be GST-free if the payment received is either less than 50% of market value of the vehicle inclusive of GST; or less than 75% of the original cost of the vehicle. When you dispose of a vehicle used to make financial supplies or use for private purpose, you may be entitled to a decreasing adjustment which reduces the amount of GST payable for the tax period. This rule on decreasing adjustment does not apply if the motor vehicle was purchased before 1 July 2000; or if it is due to the GST Transitional Act (purchased from 1 July 2000 to 23 May 2001) during which GST credits could not be claimed.

XERO

When you acquire a new depreciating asset in Xero you will need to enter it in the Fixed Asset register by going to:

Accounts>Fixed Assets>New asset

Say you bought a photocopier for $1,650 including GST and paid by cheque. You started using it on the 1st of July 2013. Assume that your bank feeds with your bank are already set up and the following day you reconciled the account. The amount to be entered in the Fixed Assets register is the amount excluding the GST. In our example it is $1,500 ($1,650 less $150 GST or $1,650/110%).

Assume that the useful life is five years. The Commissioner's determination of depreciating assets' useful lives is in TR 2013/4 available from www.ato.gov.au. That document contains the useful lives of assets in years listed per industry.

Diagram 8.1 Setting up a new Fixed Asset in Xero online accounting

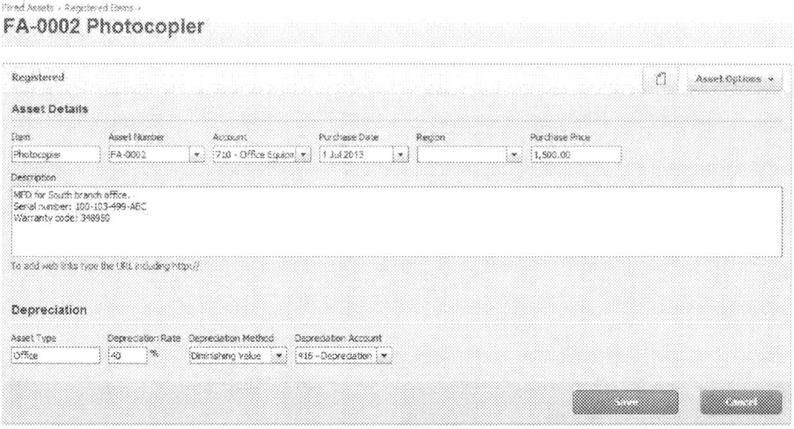

FA-0002 Photocopier

| Registered | | | | | | 🖉 | Asset Options ▾ |

Asset Details

Item	Asset Number	Account	Purchase Date	Region	Purchase Price
Photocopier	FA-0002 ▾	710 - Office Equipm ▾	1 Jul 2013 ▾	▾	1,500.00

Description

MFD for South branch office.
Serial number: 180-103-499-ABC
Warranty code: 348990

To add web links type the URL including http://

Depreciation

Asset Type	Depreciation Rate	Depreciation Method	Depreciation Account
Office	40 %	Diminishing Value ▾	415 - Depreciation ▾

Save   Cancel

Diagram 8.2   When you depreciate a Fixed Asset in Xero you need to enter the end date which is normally the end of the financial year. The path is *Accounts>Fixed Assets>Depreciation*

Demo Company (AU)

| Dashboard | Accounts ▾ | Payroll | Reports | Adviser | Contacts | Settings |

Fixed Assets >
Depreciation

📅 Start Date

Depreciate from	Depreciate to	
1 Jul 2013	30 Jun 2014 ▾	Update

There are no accounts to display.

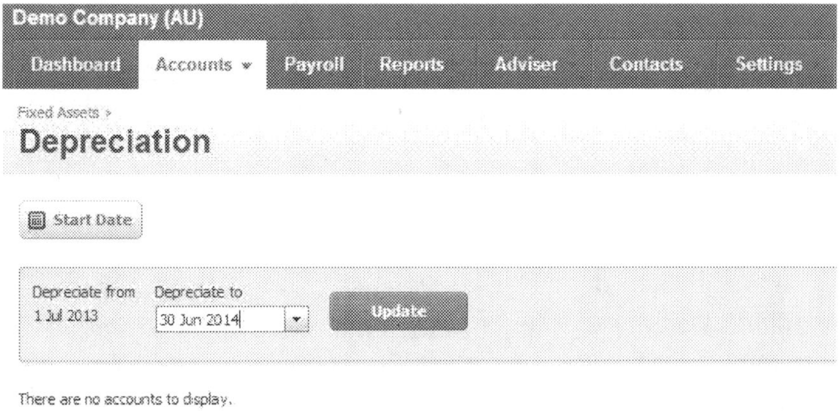

Once the asset is set up in the register in Xero, you can run the Depreciate function from the first of July until the end of the financial year. You will need to enter the end date so that Xero will automatically calculate the depreciation of the assets up until that date. Xero shows depreciation per month on the Profit and Loss report.

Diagram 8.3   **When you depreciate a Fixed Asset in Xero you need to enter the end date which is normally the end of the financial year**

MYOB

In MYOB, regardless of how you paid for the asset (whether cash, cheque or credit) the debit will still be to the fixed motor vehicle account. For example, you bought a photocopier for $1,650 including GST (or $1,500 plus GST) and issued a cheque to the supplier The Best Technologies Pty Ltd. Note that the tax code used is CAP (capital purchase). This is recorded via:

Command Centre>Banking>Spend money

Diagram 8.4 Recording the purchase of photocopier equipment in MYOB

The depreciation is recorded via the General Journal entry at the end of the year. Using our photocopier example, the depreciation entry in MYOB at the end of the year will be:

Diagram 8.5 Recording the depreciation in MYOB at the end of the year

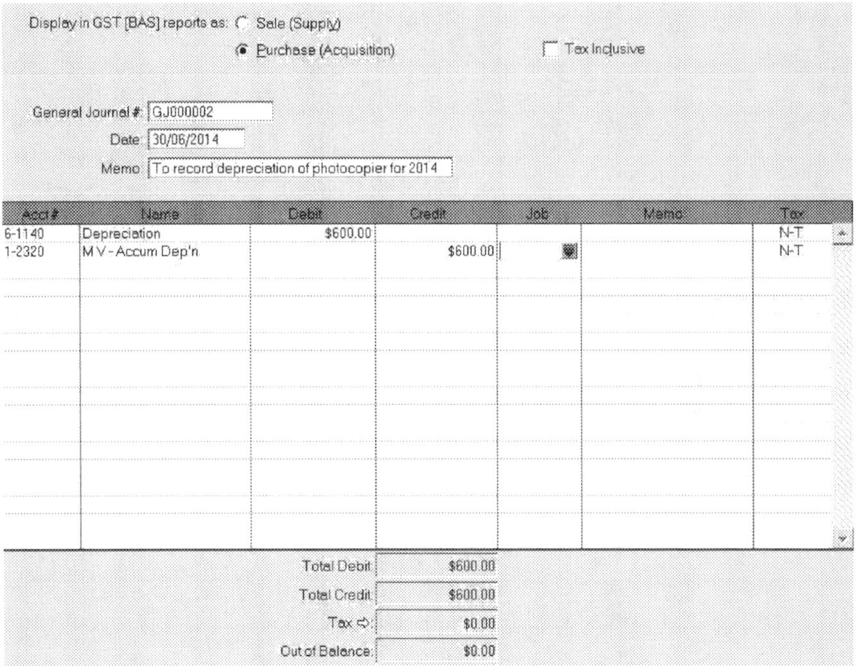

Display in GST [BAS] reports as: ○ Sale (Supply)
  ● Purchase (Acquisition)   ☐ Tax Inclusive

General Journal #: GJ000002
Date: 30/06/2014
Memo: To record depreciation of photocopier for 2014

Acct #	Name	Debit	Credit	Job	Memo	Tax
6-1140	Depreciation	$600.00				N-T
1-2320	M V - Accum Dep'n		$600.00	▓		N-T

Total Debit:	$600.00
Total Credit:	$600.00
Tax ⇨:	$0.00
Out of Balance:	$0.00

You can also record the depreciation monthly. In this case you may want to save your first entry as a recurring one so you will have the option to set up a monthly alert for example to remind you to make the entry next time you log into MYOB. When you save the first depreciation entry for the month of July 2013, you will be prompted to set up parameters for the recurring transaction. You can set select the frequency of the transaction and whether to continue indefinitely or until a specified date. You can also set up alerts to record the transaction or even automatically make the entry when upon a due date. Below are the entries in MYOB for recording depreciation. The first one is a normal monthly entry without the recurring option. You will need to remember to do this entry every month. The second one is with a recurring option.

Diagram 8.6a Recording monthly depreciation in MYOB

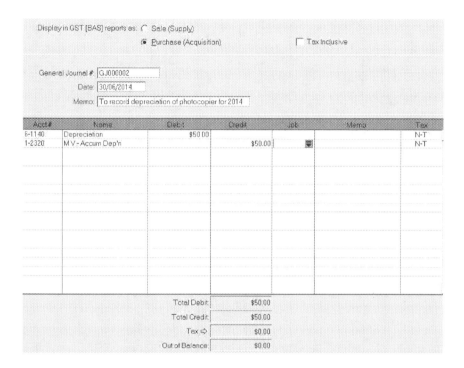

Diagram 8.6b Recording monthly depreciation in MYOB with recurring option

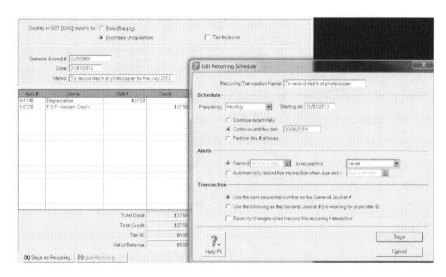

Substantiation methods

There are four substantiation methods that the Australian Taxation Office prescribes. You can use the first method if you travel less than 5,000 kilometres and the third and fourth methods if you travel more than 5,000 kilometres. The fourth method which is the log-book method is the closest to the actual motor vehicle expenses because it is based on a business percentage which in turn is based on twelve weeks that is representative of the car's business use.

1. Cents per kilometre
2. 12% of original value
3. One-third of actual expenses
4. Log book method

Cents per kilometre

This is limited to 5,000 kilometres per financial year regardless how much you have actually travelled. There is no need to keep written evidence but you need to be able to show how you calculated the kilometres. For example if you go between your clients clocking 30 kilometres each week, your average travel is 52 weeks x 30 = 1,560 kilometres. You then multiply this by a set rate based on the engine size the ATO publishes or updates every year. This may not be the best method for you if you travel more than 5,000 kilometres. Under this method you cannot make a separate claim for depreciation.

ORDINARY ENGINE CAPACITY	CENTS PER KILOMETRE
1.6 litre or less	63 cents
1.601 to 2.6 litres	74 cents
2.601 litres and over	75 cents

As per GSTB 2006/1 from the Australian Taxation Office, there is an assumed percentage of GST credit that you can claim if you use the cents per kilometre method of substantiation:

ESTIMATED KILOMETRES TRAVELLED FOR A CREDITABLE PURPOSE FOR A YEAR	ASSUMED EXTENT OF CREDITABLE PURPOSE
0 – 1250	5%
1251 – 2500	10%
2501 – 3750	15%
3751 – 5000	20%

For 12% of original value and one-third of actual expenses, the assumed creditable purpose rate is 33.33%.

12% of original value

You can only use this method if you travelled more than 5,000 kilometres during the income year. There is no need to keep written evidence but you need to be able to show how you calculated the kilometres. The amount of the claim is 12% of the original value which is basically the cost of the car or the market value if it is leased when it was first leased subject to the luxury car limit. This means it cannot exceed the luxury car limit for the income year. Under this method you cannot make a separate claim for depreciation.

One-third of actual expenses

You can only use this method if you travelled more than 5,000 kilometres during the income year. You also need to have written evidence of all your car expenses (fuel, oil, insurance, registration, repairs, interest and depreciation) and odometer readings. One-third of the total amount is the claim.

Log book method

This method requires a log book because the business percentage is worked based on the kilometres travelled relating to business out of the total kilometres travelled. You need to have log book for at least 12 continuous weeks that are representative of the car's business use. Once you have that it is valid for five years. You also need to have written evidence of all your car expenses (fuel, oil, insurance, registration, repairs, interest and depreciation) and odometer readings.

There is a lot to remember about motor vehicles but what I learned when it comes to recordkeeping is this - you can forget about everything else about motor vehicles except two things:

1. Keep a log-book for 12 continuous weeks
2. Keep written evidence of all your car expenses and odometer readings

Having done these two recording tasks you more options on how you can make claims at the end of the year.

Notes

Notes

Chapter 9

How to reconcile your accounts and prepare month-end adjustments

There are various ways to reconcile your accounts efficiently depending on whether you use Xero, MYOB or manual system. It also depends on the GST accounting method you have chosen. Regardless of which system you use keep in mind that when you do the daily tasks, the weekly tasks will be easier. When the weekly tasks are done, the monthly ones will be easier, and so forth. When the time comes to lodge your BAS the reconciliation will be minimal. And at the end of the year, if your records are organised and have your profit and loss and balance sheet produced you can probably do your own income tax return. You need to perform some end of year procedures like reviewing your inventory valuation by the 30th of June.

The best way to start the reconciliation is to have a checklist in front of you. You need to have one depending on which system you use. I have developed three sets of checklists below based on three system - Xero, MYOB and manual system. Note that there is nothing preventing you from doing the weekly tasks daily if you want to really stay on top of things particularly with bank feeds that are updated daily anyway.

XERO

DAILY	DONE
File purchases' tax invoices and receipts sorted by supplier	
File sales' tax invoices and receipts sorted per date – this would be more efficient for grocery and convenience stores where sales are made directly to consumers	
Deposit cheques and cash in the bank	
Pay by cheque or card as much as possible so there is audit trail	
If you purchase a fixed asset, enter in Fixed Asset registry and start depreciation then it will calculate monthly depreciation	
WEEKLY	
Ensure that all cheques and cash for the week are deposited in the bank	
Reconcile bank feeds (Notice that Xero suggests accounts to use based on previous transactions)	
By reconciling bank feeds you also confirm the accuracy of GST sales and GST-free before they are recorded	
By reconciling bank feeds you also confirm the accuracy of GST purchases and GST-free purchases before they are recorded	
Any transaction that comes through bank feeds need to be confirmed and recorded to the correct accounts	
Transactions not processed through the business bank account are recorded by manual journals. Examples can be uncommon transactions such as buying assets, advances to and from the business or bank loan	
Reconcile and ensure that total Xero cheque balance equals bank balance	
Ensure cash transactions are recorded via Manual Journal	
MONTHLY	
Reconcile and ensure that total Xero cheque balance equals bank balance	

Print the nine reconciliation reports and check for reasonableness and any possible errors. The nine reports are: 1. Trial Balance 2. Aged Receivables 3. Aged Payables 4. Business Bank Account Reconciliation 5. Business Savings Account Reconciliation 6. GST Reconciliation 7. Fixed Asset Reconciliation 8. General Ledger Exceptions 9. Journal Report	
Check that the total card payment matches with total of specific invoices (refer to Chapter 5 about credit card payments)	
Print the Profit and loss statement and check for reasonableness of amounts and any possible errors	
Check if there are prepayments that need to be amortised	
Keep track of the cheques that have been cleared	
Save softcopies of monthly Profit and Loss report, Balance Sheet, and Trial Balance in both PDF and CSV on your computer	
QUARTERLY	
Print Activity Statement report for the quarter in Xero and review	
Log into your Business Portal and follow the prompts to lodge your BAS for the relevant quarter	
Save a softcopy of the BAS you have lodged	
Save softcopies of quarterly Profit and Loss report, Balance Sheet, and Trial Balance in both PDF and CSV on your computer	
YEARLY	
Reconcile four quarterly BAS for the financial year against your total figures for the year ensuring that they all match	

Perform payroll procedures if applicable (refer to www.xero.com)	
Print the nine reconciliation reports for the year and check for reasonableness and any possible errors before closing off the year	

Note: Use the Xero support forum if you need assistance. This is closely monitored by a Xero consultant so make use of it. Google Xero support

MYOB

DAILY	DONE
Add up all the GST sales and GST-free sales from your cash register sales summary and record	
Ensure that you have recorded the other income	
Ensure that you have recorded the purchases you received the tax invoice or paid for	
Record other expenses (and related GST if applicable)	
Record uncommon transactions such as buying assets, advances to and from the business or bank loan	
WEEKLY	
Ensure that all cheques and cash for the week are deposited in the bank	
Ensure cash transactions are recorded either via Record Journal Entry or Spend money (but under a cash account not a cheque account)	
MONTHLY	
Reconcile bank by going to *Banking>Reconcile Accounts*	

Run seven out of eight of exception reports and reconcile The eight reports are:
  1. Payables Reconciliation
  2. Receivables Reconciliation
  3. Payroll Liabilities Reconciliation
  4. Tax Code Reconciliation
  5. Future Dated Transactions
  6. Prepaid Transactions
  7. Deposit Transactions	

Check that the total card payment matches with total of specific invoices (refer to Chapter 5 about credit card payments)	
Print the Profit and loss statement and check for reasonableness of amounts and any possible errors	
Keep track of the cheques that have been cleared	
Save softcopies of monthly Profit and Loss report, Balance Sheet, and Trial Balance in both PDF and CSV on your computer	
QUARTERLY	
Run the Inventory Valuation Reconciliation which is one of the exception reports in MYOB	
Run the *BASlink* for the quarter via the Command Centre and review	
Log into your Business Portal and follow the prompts to lodge your BAS for the relevant quarter	
Save a softcopy of the BAS you have lodged	
YEARLY	
Reconcile four quarterly BAS for the financial year against your total figures for the year ensuring that they all match	
Perform payroll procedures if applicable refer to www.myob.com.au	

Perform year-end procedures including new PAYG tax table for the next financial year and other updates. MYOB sends yearly updates in CD	

Note: Use the *Help* menu if you are in doubt. You can also use the MYOB forum where users and consultants share their expertise and help solve your queries

MANUAL

DAILY	DONE
File purchases' tax invoices and receipts sorted by supplier	
File sales' tax invoices and receipts sorted per date – this would be more efficient for grocery and convenience stores where sales are made directly to consumers	
Deposit cheques and cash in the bank – your bank statement almost serves as your accounting system so put all business transactions into your business account	
Pay by cheque or card as much as possible so there is audit trail	
If you purchase a fixed asset, enter in Fixed Asset registry including information on purchase date, sale price or market value, useful life	
Ensure cash transactions are recorded	
WEEKLY	
Keep track of the following every week otherwise there will be a huge build-up at the end of the month if you use a manual system 1. Aged Payables (with number of days outstanding) 2. Aged Receivables (with number of days outstanding) 3. Payroll Liabilities Reconciliation 4. Prepaid Transactions 5. GST reconciliation 6. General Journal entries	

MONTHLY	
Perform manual bank reconciliation (you can download template from www.accountsunplugged.com)	
Check that the total card payment matches with total of specific invoices (refer to Chapter 5 about credit card payments)	
Prepare and print the Profit and loss statement and check for reasonableness of amounts and any possible errors	
Keep track of the cheques that have been cleared	
Prepare and print monthly Profit and Loss report, Balance Sheet, and Trial Balance. Save softcopies of these reports in both PDF and CSV on your computer	
QUARTERLY	
Use the GST worksheet sent to you by the ATO before completing the final BAS	
Log into your Business Portal and follow the prompts to lodge your BAS for the relevant quarter	
Save a softcopy of the BAS you have lodged	
Save softcopies of quarterly Profit and Loss report, Balance Sheet, and Trial Balance in both PDF and CSV on your computer	
YEARLY	
Print and review fixed asset register and update depreciation expense and accumulated depreciation of your depreciating assets. Save a softcopy on your computer	
Reconcile four quarterly BAS for the financial year against your total figures for the year ensuring that they all match	
Perform payroll procedures	
Print weekly reports this time for the whole year and check for reasonableness and any possible errors before closing off the year	

Note: If possible make it your aim to use some sort of a double entry or accounting system like MYOB or Xero. They are getting affordable and available on different subscription plans depending on your needs

If you are using Xero, the first reconciliation you do is the bank. When you log into you Xero account, go to **Accounts>Bank Accounts** and click on the blue *Reconcile items* button.

Diagram 9.1 Adviser Reports in Xero include Reconciliation Reports

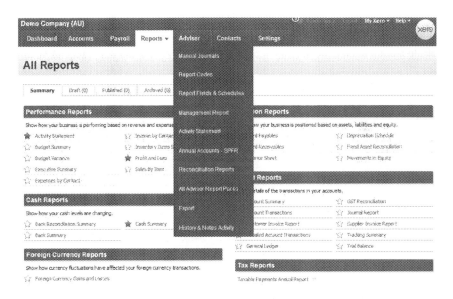

Diagram 9.2a   Adviser Reports in Xero include Reconciliation Reports before running update

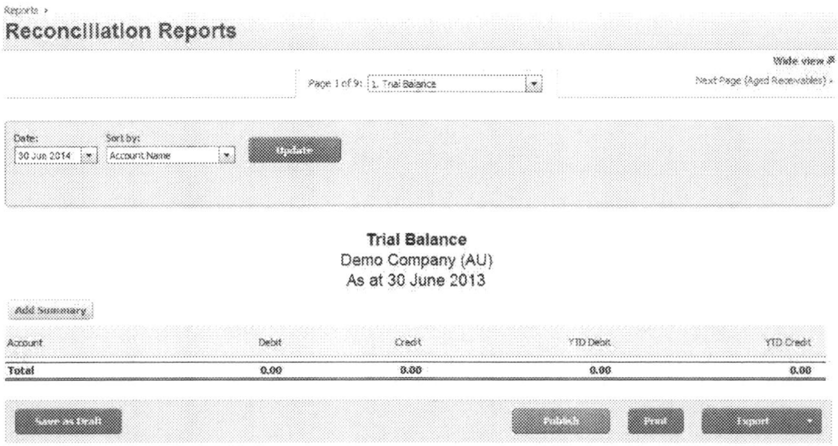

Diagram 9.2b Trial Balance in Reconciliation Reports after running update

Trial Balance
Demo Company (AU)
As at 30 June 2014

Add Summary

Account	Debit	Credit	YTD Debit	YTD Credit
Revenue				
Interest Income (270)		0.00		97.85
Sales (200)		0.00		45,151.05
Expenses				
Advertising (400)	0.00		4,107.91	
Bank Fees (404)	0.00		331.50	
Cleaning (408)	0.00		463.00	
Consulting & Accounting (412)	0.00		98.00	
Depreciation (416)	263.02		2,573.15	
Entertainment (420)	0.00		277.20	
Freight & Courier (425)	0.00			9.09
General Expenses (429)	0.00		1,085.05	
Legal expenses (441)	0.00		4,190.91	
Light, Power, Heating (445)	0.00		1,544.73	
Motor Vehicle Expenses (449)	0.00		878.98	
Office Expenses (453)	0.00		1,423.92	
Printing & Stationery (461)	0.00		180.45	
Purchases (300)	0.00		753.64	
Rent (469)	0.00		5,373.86	
Subscriptions (485)	0.00		125.00	
Telephone & Internet (489)	0.00		239.56	
Travel - National (493)	0.00		582.14	
Wages and Salaries (477)	0.00		40,200.00	

Diagram 9.3 Nine reconciliation reports available in Xero

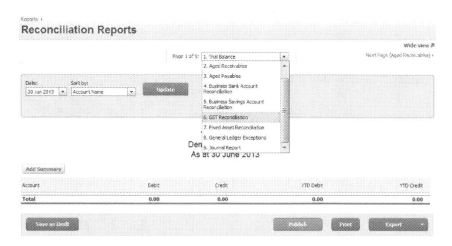

Diagram 9.4 Reconciling bank feeds in Xero

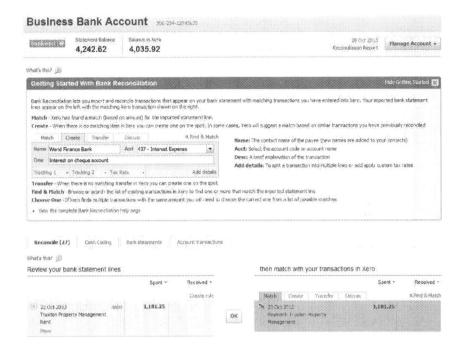

You can see on the diagram that Xero already proposes a match of the bank statement line from your bank on the left-hand side with an entry in you Xero. If you approve the suggested match, click OK. When reconciling bank feeds in Xero, keep the following in mind:

1. Determine if there is GST or not or if the transaction is input-taxed
2. Work out the amount of the GST of the transaction and record it separately
3. At the end of the day, you need to know the total figures of at least the following:

   a. Total sales with GST
   b. Total sales that are GST free

    c. Sales that are input-taxed
    d. Purchases with GST
    e. Purchases that are GST free
    f. Purchases that are input-taxed

4. If it has something to do with assets, liabilities or equity (balance sheet accounts) determine the specific accounts to be used

5. If you get stuck or unsure about anything, go online by clicking the *Help* link at the top right of the page you are having difficulties with. Most probably you will find answers to your Xero questions otherwise post your question and either the Xero moderator or Xero online user will respond with a possible solution. You can also subscribe to Accounts Unplugged's BAS accountant online

6. Ensure that corrections from previous quarter are corrected in the current one (observe time limit per ATO)

Notes

Notes

Chapter 10

How to prepare and lodge your BAS

Before we go into the details of setting the *BASlink* in MYOB or generating the Activity Statement report in Xero, below is the list of BAS labels and items included under each label. We also show you snippets of a sample Business Activity Statement from www.ato.gov.au. Take time to familiarise yourself with these items particularly the ones that apply to you. Please note that input tax credits also mean GST credits; sales also mean supplies; purchases also mean acquisition; and business means enterprise.

Diagram 10.1a Example of a quarterly Business Activity Statement (front) from www.ato.gov.au

FRONT

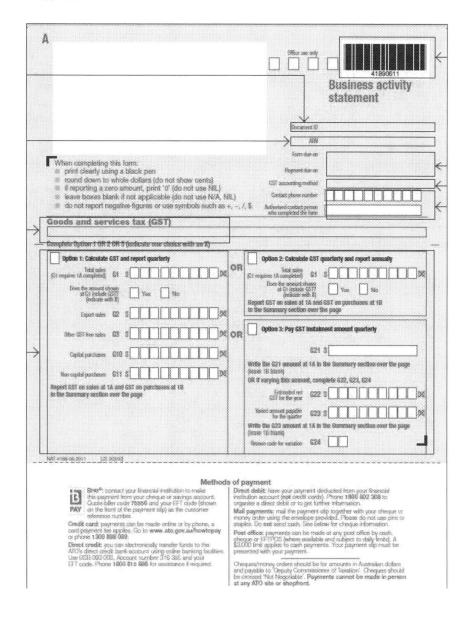

Diagram 10.1b Example of a quarterly Business Activity Statement (back) from www.ato.gov.au

BACK

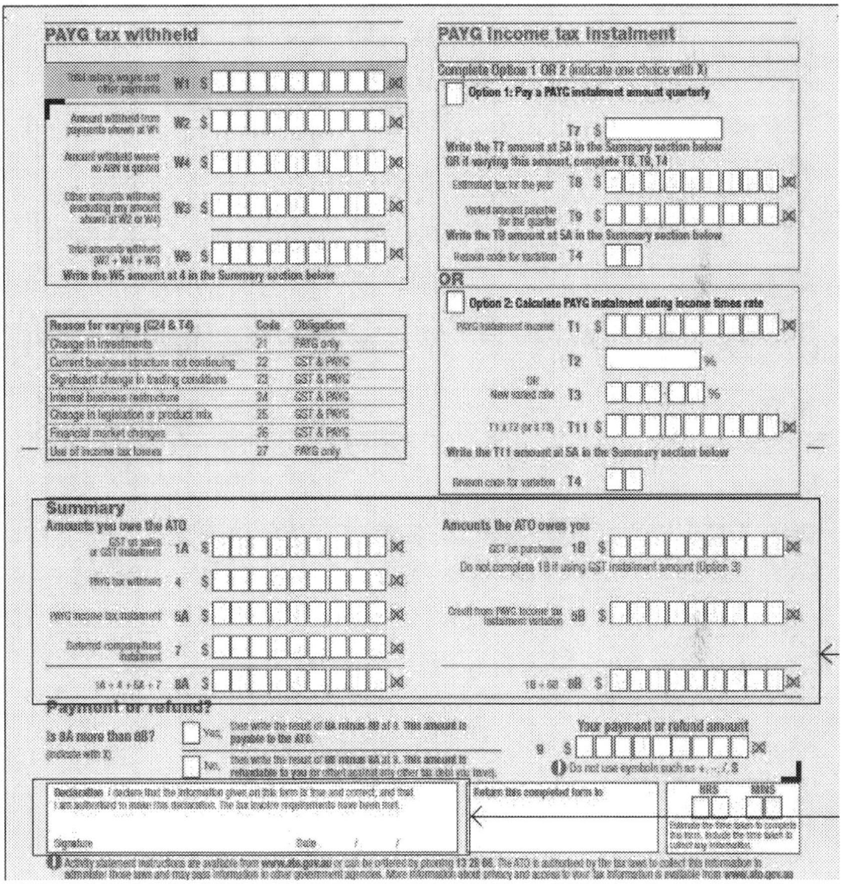

PAYG tax withheld

Total salary, wages and other payments W1 $

Amount withheld from payments shown at W1 W2 $

Amount withheld where no ABN is quoted W4 $

Other amounts withheld (excluding any amount shown at W2 or W4) W3 $

Total amounts withheld (W2 + W4 + W3) W5 $

Write the W5 amount at 4 in the Summary section below

Reason for varying (G24 & T4)	Code	Obligation
Change in investments	21	PAYG only
Current business structure not continuing	22	GST & PAYG
Significant change in trading conditions	23	GST & PAYG
Internal business restructure	24	GST & PAYG
Change in legislation or product mix	25	GST & PAYG
Financial market changes	26	GST & PAYG
Use of income tax losses	27	PAYG only

PAYG income tax instalment

Complete Option 1 OR 2 (indicate one choice with X)

Option 1: Pay a PAYG instalment amount quarterly

T7 $

Write the T7 amount at 5A in the Summary section below
OR if varying this amount, complete T8, T9, T4

Estimated tax for the year T8 $

Varied amount payable for the quarter T9 $

Write the T9 amount at 5A in the Summary section below

Reason code for variation T4

OR

Option 2: Calculate PAYG instalment using income times rate

PAYG instalment income T1 $

T2 %

OR New varied rate T3 %

T1 x T2 (or x T3) T11 $

Write the T11 amount at 5A in the Summary section below

Reason code for variation T4

Summary

Amounts you owe the ATO

GST on sales or GST instalment 1A $

PAYG tax withheld 4 $

PAYG income tax instalment 5A $

Deferred company/fund instalment 7 $

1A + 4 + 5A + 7 8A $

Amounts the ATO owes you

GST on purchases 1B $

Do not complete 1B if using GST instalment amount (Option 3)

Credit from PAYG income tax instalment variation 5B $

1B + 5B 8B $

Payment or refund?

Is 8A more than 8B? (indicate with X)

Yes, then write the result of 8A minus 8B at 9. This amount is payable to the ATO.

No, then write the result of 8B minus 8A at 9. This amount is refundable to you (or offset against any other tax debt you have).

Your payment or refund amount

9 $

Do not use symbols such as +, –, /, $

Declaration I declare that the information given on this form is true and correct, and that I am authorised to make this declaration. The tax invoice requirements have been met.

Signature Date / /

Return this completed form to

HRS MINS

Estimate the time taken to complete this form. Include the time taken to collect any information.

Diagram 10.2 Example of a GST calculation worksheet from www.ato.gov.au

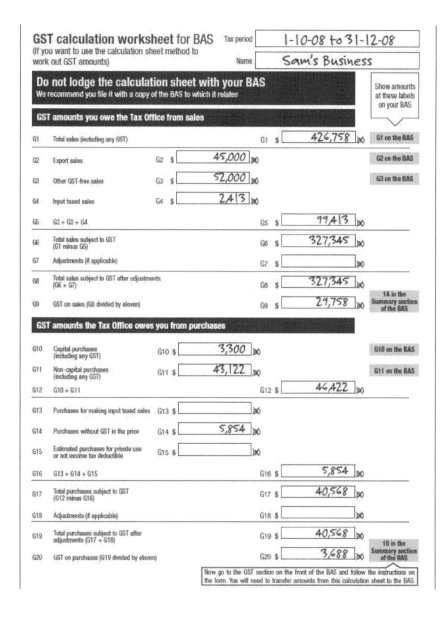

G1 - Total sales

Amounts to include

Include total sales (including those declared at G2, G3 and G4).

If you have registered to use cash basis for your GST you must include all payments you have received during the tax period for sales you have made in the course of your business. If you use accrual or non-cash, include the amount of the invoice or the cash receipt for the sale whichever comes first during that tax period.

You need to include as part of your total sales all cash payments made out of the cash register or till for stocks and supplies purchases, wages and other expenses. This is because the money you used to pay for those purchases came from your cash sales that you have not yet recorded. If you already have a system to record cash sales you do not need to record the purchases as sales otherwise, you will be recording the sales twice.

The sale price of taxable business assets is also included at **G1** and the GST amount at **1A**. The margin for the supply of a property sold under a margin scheme is also included in G1. Under a margin scheme the GST is one-eleventh of the margin rather than the normal sale price. You do not to worry about margin scheme unless you sell or will sell property in which case you may want to consider it. For more information about this scheme ring the ATO on 13 28 66.

When you sell your business include the sale price at **G1** and report the GST amount in **1A**. If it is a GST-free sale of a going concern, include the sale at **G1** and also at **G3**.

Amounts NOT to include

Do not include

- Salary and wages
- Dividends
- Loans
- Bank transfers
- Private money
- Amounts received by a company for issuing share
- Distributions from trust and partnerships
- Donations and gifts received
- Receipts from hobby activities
- Government allowances
- Tax refunds
- Income of other entities that have their own separate Australian Business Number (ABN)
- Sales not connected with Australia unless specifically included by a special rule

REMINDER: If the total amount reported at **G1** includes GST, remember to indicate with **X** in the YES box beneath the **G1** label. If you indicate NO, ensure to remove the GST amount reported at **G1**. Many businesses do include the GST at **G1** and indicate **X** in the YES box. This is actually consistent with the use of the GST worksheet provided by the ATO.

G2 - Export sales

Amounts to include

- The value of the export goods also called free on board value (without insurance or freight added) used for Customs purposes if the export is GST-free because:

1. The goods are exported from Australia within 60 days after either
   - the day you receive any payment for the sale or
   - when you issue an invoice for the sale before you receive any payment (there are some circumstances in which the purchaser can export the goods instead of you)

2. The goods are sold and the payment was to be provided as instalments under a contract that requires the goods to be exported and you exported them before or within 60 days after
   - the day on which you received any of the final instalment or
   - the day you issue an invoice for the final instalment before you receive any of the final instalment (there are some circumstances in which the purchaser can export the goods instead of you)

3. You sell an aircraft or ship that was paid for in instalments under a contract that requires the aircraft or ship to be exported, but only if the purchaser exports it from Australia within 60 days after the earliest day in which at least one of the following occurs
   - you receive any of the final instalment of payment for the sale
   - you issue an invoice for that final instalment
   - you deliver the aircraft or ship to the purchaser or (at the purchaser's request) to another person

4. You sell an aircraft or ship, but only if the purchaser exports it from Australia under its own power within 60 days after taking physical possession of it

5. You sell a ship, but only if:
   - the ship is a new recreational boat
   - you or the purchaser export the ship within 12 months, and
   - the ship is used only for recreational/non-commercial purposes while it is in Australia

6. You sell aircraft or ships stores or spare parts for use, consumption or sale on international flights or voyages, whether or not part of the flight or voyage involves a journey between places in Australia

7. Sale of goods used in the repair, renovation, modification or treatment of other goods from outside Australia and their destination is outside Australia. The goods must be attached to (or become part of) the other goods or become unusable or worthless as a direct result of being used to repair, renovate, modify or treat the other goods

8. Repair, renovation, modification or treatment of goods from overseas whose destination is outside Australia after the repair, renovation, modification or treatment

9. Sale of goods that satisfy certain criteria and are exported by travellers as accompanied baggage

Amounts NOT to include

- GST-free services unless they relate to the repair, renovation, modification or treatment of goods from overseas and their destination is outside Australia

- Freight and insurance to transport the goods outside Australia, or other charges imposed outside Australia in the free on board value
- International transport of goods or international transport of passengers
- Goods that are used in Australia
- Sales of which you are not the exporter

  Goods that did not end up being exported within 60 days you either receiving any payment for the goods, or from when you issue an invoice for the goods. You need to account for the GST in this case

The relevant rulings available from the ATO are:

- GSTR 2002/6 *Goods and services tax: exports of goods, items 1 to 4 of the table in Subsection 38-180(1) of the New Tax System (Goods and Services Tax) Act 1999*
- GSTR 2003/4 *Goods and services tax: stores and spares for international flights and voyages*
- GSTR 2005/2 *Goods and services tax: supplies of goods and services in the repair, renovation, modification or treatment of goods from outside Australia, whose destination is outside Australia.*

For those who want to extend the 60-day limit for export of your goods, ships or aircraft, you can phone the ATO on 13 28 66.

G3 – Other GST-free sales

Amounts to include

- basic food
- education and health services

- certain childcare services
- beverages (including water) for human consumption listed in Schedule 2 of *A New Tax System (Goods and Services Tax) Act 1999*
- eligible childcare services
- certain sales by eligible charities, gift deductible entities or government schools where specific conditions are satisfied, including sales for a token amount of payment and raffles and bingo
- sales made to a resident of a retirement village by an eligible charity of accommodation in a retirement village or services relating to the supply of that accommodation and the provision of meals
- religious services provided by religious institutions that are integral to practicing that religion
- sales of going concerns -certain conditions must be satisfied including that you and the purchaser have agreed in writing that the sale is of a going concern and you supply all things necessary for the continued operation of the business
- the first sale of precious metal after its refining by, or on behalf of, the seller, and:
  1. it was refined by a precious metal refiner, and
  2. the sale was made to a dealer in precious metal

- sales of water (except if it is provided in, or transferred into, containers with a capacity of less than 100 litres)
- certain sewerage services including emptying of septic tanks and storm water draining
- international transport and mail that meets certain criteria (phone 13 28 66 for more information)
- certain services in arranging international travel

Amounts NOT to include

- sales included at G2
- basic food, including food for human consumption that is
  1. for consumption on the premises from which it is sold (for example, cafes and restaurants)
  2. hot takeaway food
  3. a food type listed in Schedule 1 of *A New Tax System (Goods and Services Tax) Act 1999* (certain prepared food, confectionery, savoury snacks, bakery products, ice cream foods and biscuits) or foods that are a combination of foods where at least one food type in the combination is listed in Schedule 1

- sales of water that are provided in, or transferred into, containers with a capacity of less than 100 litres

<u>G4 – Input-taxed sales</u>

Amounts to include

- financial supplies
- renting or leasing residential premises that are to be used predominantly for residential accommodation (that is, they are not commercial residential premises) as long as the lease is not a long-term lease
- sales of residential premises that are to be used predominantly for residential accommodation (that is, they are not commercial residential premises or new residential premises)

Amounts NOT to include

- long-term leases of residential premises
- new residential premises that were not used for residential accommodation before 2 December 1998. This includes premises that have been substantially renovated – these should be reported at G1

G5 – Subtotal of G2 + G3 + G4

This label is the total of the GST-free and input taxed sales

G6 – Total sales subject to GST

Total of G1 decreased by the amount at G5. This is the total of your taxable sales.

G7 – Adjustments

Include adjustments that increase the net amount of GST payable. An example of this is when you sell goods that are GST-free for export but ended up not exported, therefore become taxable.

G10 – Capital purchases

Amounts to include

- amounts for capital items such as
  1. machinery and equipment
  2. cash registers
  3. office furniture
  4. computers
  5. cars

- the GST-inclusive market value of any capital item you receive from your associate for no payment or for less than the GST-inclusive market value, if either:
  1. you have not received the thing wholly or partly for your business
  2. the thing received is wholly or partly of a private or domestic nature
  3. the thing received relates wholly or partly to making sales that would be input taxed.

Note: For purchases for $1,000 or less, G10 (and G11) require you to separately report your capital and non-capital purchases. If you already record these purchases separately in your records, use this existing breakdown to fill in the G10 and G11 labels. If you do not record capital and non-capital purchases separately and your GST turnover is expected to be less than $1 million then:

- you only need to record capital items costing more than $1,000 at G10 (capital purchases)
- capital and non-capital items costing $1,000 or less can be recorded at G11 (non-capital purchases)

G11 - Non-capital purchases

Amounts to include

All amounts for your business purchases (other than those reported at G10) relevant to the reporting period such as:

1. most business purchases, including services and stock bought for resale, office supplies, equipment rentals or leases
2. commercial rent or rent of property from another person to carry on a business assuming both lessee and lessor are GST-registered

3. the price of any insurance premiums related to your business (except for third-party motor insurance premiums relating to a period of cover starting before 1 July 2003) less the amount of stamp duty
4. purchases paid for by an employee, agent, officer or partner that you have reimbursed in specified circumstances
5. capital items costing $1,000 or less that have not been reported at G10
6. intangible supplies purchased from off-shore that are of a non-capital nature

The GST-inclusive market value of any non-capital item you receive from your associate for no payment or for less than the GST-inclusive market value, if either:

- You have not received the thing wholly or partly for your business the thing received is wholly or partly of a private, or
- domestic nature the thing received relates wholly or partly to making supplies that would be input taxed

Amounts NOT to include at G11

- purchases and importations that are not related to your business
- an amount for a purchase or importation of a car that exceeds the car limit for the relevant financial year, unless you are specifically entitled to quote an ABN in relation to the supply to which the purchase relates or in relation to the importation
- the price of any third-party motor insurance premiums relating to a period of cover starting before 1 July 2003
- anything that is constituted by an insurer settling a claim under an insurance policy or by an operator of a compulsory third-party scheme settling a claim under a compulsory third-party scheme (if you are not an operator of such a scheme)

- salary and wages you pay
- superannuation contributions you pay for employees

G13 – Purchases for making input taxed sales

Amounts to include

- amounts for purchases and importations, but only for the part or amount that relates to making sales that would be input taxed sales (see G4 for examples of input taxed sales)
- if you received anything from an associate for no payment, or you have paid less than the full GST-inclusive market value, you must
- work out what portion of it relates to making sales that would be input taxed
- report that portion of its full GST-inclusive market value at G13

Amounts NOT to include at G13

You do not report at G13 amounts for purchases or importations that relate to making financial supplies and you do not exceed the financial acquisitions threshold

G14 – Purchases without GST in the price

Amounts to include

- amounts for purchases and importations that did not have GST included in the price. This includes sales to you that were
  1. GST-free or input taxed (G2, G3 or G4)
  2. made by an entity not registered for GST
  3. not connected with Australia (and not taxable)

4. non-taxable importations
5. intangible supplies purchased from off-shore that are not subject to a GST reverse charge.

- payments of Australian taxes, fees and charges where GST was not included in the price charged

G15 – Estimated purchases for private use or not income tax deductible

Amounts to include

- amounts for purchases and importations that are of a private or domestic nature – if a purchase or importation was only partly of a private or domestic nature, you must
    1. work out what amount of the purchase or importation was of a private or domestic nature
    2. only report that amount at G15

- anything you received from an associate for no payment or for less than the GST-inclusive market value – in these cases you must work out what portion of the thing is of a private or domestic nature report that amount of the GST-inclusive market value of the thing at G15
- purchases or importations that are not income tax deductible, including
    1. expenses for maintaining your family
    2. penalties
    3. uniforms (if they are not compulsory or protective clothing)
    4. entertainment expenses, except where the expenses are incurred in providing a fringe benefit
    5. travel expenses for relatives, except where the expenses are incurred in providing a fringe benefit

6. recreational club expenses, except where the expenses are incurred in providing a fringe benefit

7. expenses for leisure facility or boat, except where the expenses are incurred in providing a fringe benefit

8. expenses you incur under an agreement for providing non-deductible non-cash business benefits (up to the arm's length value of that benefit).

- any portion of the following purchases and importations that are non-deductible for income tax purposes

  1. expenses incurred when providing meal entertainment if for fringe benefit tax purposes you use either the 50/50 split method or the 12-week register method to determine the taxable value of meal entertainment fringe benefits

  2. entertainment facility leasing expenses if for fringe benefit tax purposes, you use the 50/50 split method in relation to these expenses

- if you are eligible and have made a valid annual apportionment election, report at G15 amounts for your private portion of purchases and importations subject to the election.

G16 – Subtotal of G13 + G14 + G15

Add amounts at G13 (purchases for making input taxed sales), G14 (purchases without GST in the price) and G15 (estimated purchases for private use or not income tax deductible). This total amount is the portion of the purchases and importations that you cannot claim GST for.

G17 – Total purchases subject to GST

Subtracting G16 from G12 gives you the amount that represents the portion that you can claim GST credits for.

G18 – Adjustments

Include decreasing adjustments at this label.

G19 – Total purchases subject to GST after adjustments

Add G17 and G18 and you will get the final total purchases subject to GST.

G20 – GST on purchases

Divide G19 (final total purchases subject to GST) by 11. This amount is also at label 1B.

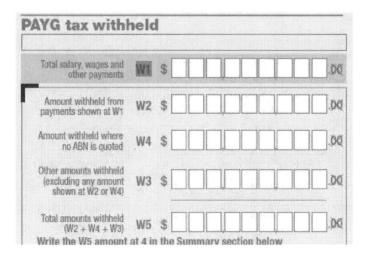

Diagram 10.3 PAYG tax withheld section of the BAS

W1 Total salary, wages and other payments

These are gross payments from which you are required to withhold amounts. They include:

- salary and wages, fees and allowances paid to employees and directors
- salary and allowances paid to office holders, including members of parliament, defence force members and police officers
- leave payments
- payments made by a labour hire firm to workers under a labour hire agreement
- employment termination payments
- payments made to religious practitioners
- Commonwealth education and training payments

Note that they DO NOT include:

- salary sacrifice amounts
- superannuation contribution
- payments from which an amount was withheld because no ABN was quoted (these payments are included in W4)
- interest, dividends or royalty payments made to non-residents that you withheld amounts from
- distributions from which amounts were withheld because no TFN was quoted
- payments made to foreign residents for sports, entertainment, casino gaming junket activities and construction
- DASP (departing Australia superannuation payments)

Note: If there are no payments, leave labels blank. Also if you are a large withholder ($1 million in a previous income year), you only need to complete **W1**. Do not complete **W2**, **W3**, **W4**, **W5** and **4** in the *Summary* section.

W2 - Amounts withheld from salaries or wages and other payments shown at W1

This is the total amount withheld from the payments shown at **W1**. If there are no withheld amounts label blank

W4 - Amounts withheld where no ABN is quoted

This is the total amount withheld from payments made to suppliers who did not quote their ABN. If there are no withheld amounts label blank

W3 - Other amounts withheld (excluding any amount shown at W2 or W4)

This includes all other types of withholding not shown on **W1** and **W2**. Examples of these payments include:

- interest, dividends or royalty payments you made to a non-resident
- payments made to a non-resident (interest, dividends, royalty) where the person has not completed a Tax File Number declaration form (form code is NAT3092).
- payments made to foreign residents for sports, entertainment, casino gaming junket activities and construction
- DASP (departing Australia superannuation payments)

Note that if you have nothing to report at these label, leave it blank.

W5 - Total amounts withheld (W2 + W4 + W3)

This is the total of W2, W4 and W3. Copy the total at this label to label 4 in the Summary section of the BAS. If the BAS only asks to report PAYG withholding, there will be no *Summary* section. The total withholding will be reported at 9 in the *Payment* or *Refund* section

4 - PAYG tax withheld (summary section)

Copy the total from W5 to 4 in the **Summary** section of the BAS

1A – GST on sales or GST instalment

Include at this label the total amount of GST that is payable for the reporting BAS period. If you use Xero online accounting and assuming your chart of accounts are set up correctly with correct tax codes, the activity statement report produces the figures of all the relevant labels you need to report on your actual BAS. Generating the report takes a few seconds. All the work was already done during the set up stage and the recording transactions either daily or weekly. It is even less work if you use Xero online accounting where bank feeds can be set up transactions are fed into your Xero account and Xero tries to match the feeds with suppliers and accounts that you have used from your previous transactions. All you need to do is match the transactions that were fed clicking OK. This saves you hours in keying transactions. Online accounting is further discussed in Chapter 5. If you are using MYOB and the *BASlink* is set up, you generate the BAS worksheet and transfer the figures across the actual BAS to be lodged.

The amount reported at 1A depends on the option chosen of the three provided by the ATO. The options again are in Chapter 2 BAS obligations.

Below is a list of the reasons for varying the amount of PAYG instalment in the BAS provided by the ATO on www.ato.gov.au. This reason is shown at label **T4**.

Diagram 10.4 Reasons for varying PAYG amount

Reason code	Reason for varying PAYG amount	Description and examples
21	Change in investments	Your investment strategy or policy has changed and this will significantly affect your annual tax liability. For example: • the sale or purchase of investments such as shares or residential property • the use of investments for private purposes • when moving from the accumulation phase to pension phase for your superannuation benefits.
22	Current business structure not continuing	Your current business has stopped trading or has changed its structure. For example, your business has: • permanently closed or been sold • stopped trading because of a merger or takeover • gone into bankruptcy or liquidation • have been placed in the hands of a receiver/manager.

23	Significant change in trading conditions	Abnormal transactions relating to your business income or expenses will significantly affect your annual tax liability. For example: • you have bought or sold a major piece of machinery • your trading conditions have been affected by local or global competition.
24	Internal business restructure	You have restructured your business. For example, it has undergone an expansion or contraction, which will significantly affect your annual tax liability.
25	Change in legislation or product mix	A change in legislation, or the product mix of your business, will significantly change your annual tax liability.
26	Financial market changes	Your business is involved in financial market trading and has been affected by domestic or foreign financial market changes. This includes businesses whose income is affected by changes in financial products, such as banks and finance and insurance businesses.
27	Use of income tax losses	You will be using income tax losses, including capital losses transferred from another entity that will significantly affect your annual tax liability.

33	Consolidations	A head company can vary its consolidated instalment based on its estimate of the expected consolidation outcomes for the year. When varying as a result of consolidation, use the special variation code 33 on the consolidated activity statement.

OTHER BAS REMINDERS

1. The only time you do not have to lodge is when you receive an instalment notice. Instalment notices have the letter N, R, S or T in the top left-hand corner and a pre-printed instalment amount to pay by the due date
2. If your business turnover is $20 million or more, you must lodge your activity statement monthly.
3. If your turnover is less than this, you may still choose to lodge electronically. For more information about electronic lodgment
4. You must provide a contact name and a daytime phone number on your activity statement.
5. You must also sign and date your activity statement before you lodge it
6. If you have nothing to report in any part of your activity statement (a nil statement), you must place zeros at **1A**, **1B** and **9**. Do not write 'nil', 'n/a' or 'not applicable' anywhere on your statement.
7. Generally, you only leave boxes blank on your activity statement if they do not apply to your business. For example, if you do not have exports to report, leave the box at **G2** blank.
8. Write zero at:

    a. **G1** and **1A** if you are using GST option 1 or option 2 and you have not traded for a tax period, and you have nothing to report

    b. **T1** and **5A** if you are using PAYG option 2 but you do not have any instalment income

    c. **1A** if you are varying your GST instalment to zero

    d. **5A** if you are varying your PAYG instalment to zero.

9. You must show only whole dollars when completing your activity statement. Cents are left out and should not be rounded up to the next dollar

10. Do not use decimal points, commas, symbols such as $, words such 'NIL' or 'N/A'

11. You must only use a black pen to complete your activity statement

12. You must only complete the boxes on your activity statement for one option

Set up *BASlink*

These days of competitive environment as well as never-ending list of government requirements pose challenges to business owners not only in getting and keeping clients but also on having systems in place to comply with legal requirements. One of the ways to keep on top of things is to automate as many things as possible particularly administration to keep manual handling as low as possible. This will give you more time on things like developing promotional campaigns to acquire new clients or programs that benefit existing ones.

BASlink parameters are in *BASlink* in the main *Command Centre* menu. Ensure that company information is correct in the *Setup* menu and also the *BAS Info* before setting up the parameters in

BASlink. Once that is done, go to the main Command Centre and click on the *BASlink* on the right-hand side.

Diagram 10.5 *Setup>Company Information>BAS Info*

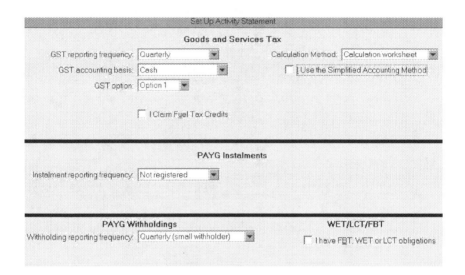

Most businesses report quarterly BAS which is probably a wise decision because it makes you reconcile your accounts regularly if not monthly, at least quarterly. Not only will you be working towards your BAS but also to keep track of your business performance, rather than wait until the end of the year which may be a bit too late to make business decisions. The GST accounting method in the *BAS info* should match the one registered with the ATO.

Diagram 10.6 *Command Centre>BASlink*

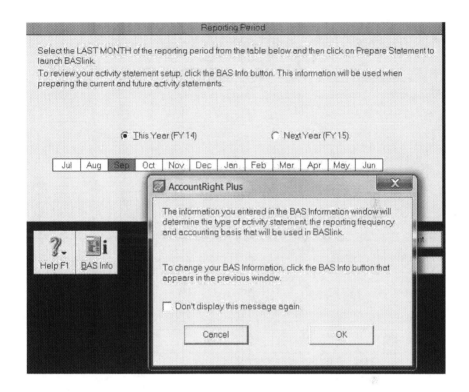

When you click on *Prepare Statement,* a message will pop saying that what you entered in the *BAS Info* window will determine the type of activity statement, the reporting frequency and accounting basis for the *BASlink.* When you click OK, you will get a DISCLAIMER message. When you get to the set up page below you will notice that there are three tabs – GST Worksheet, Front sheet and Back sheet. Spend time with the GST Worksheet to set it up correctly ensuring that you only include for example total sales in G1 (GST sales with tax code GST, GST free with tax code FRE and export sales with tax code EXP).

Diagram 10.7 GST worksheet BAS in MYOB as part of *BASlink* setup

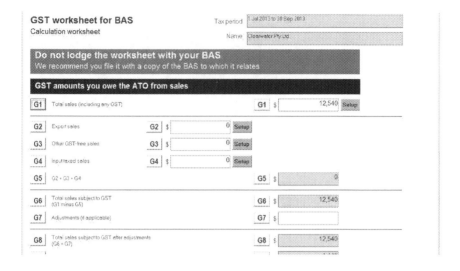

Diagram 10.8 GST worksheet BAS in MYOB as part of *BASlink* setup

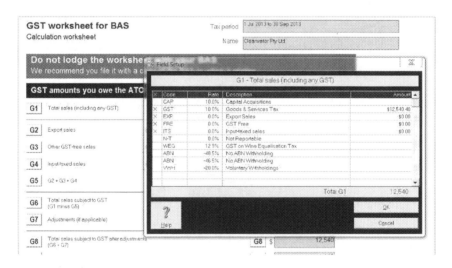

G2 Export Sales needs to have a separate tax code set up if you do make export sales. You can set up a new tax code via the *List* menu *(List>Tax Codes).* Click the New button at the bottom middle part of the window. For example, we set up a code called

EXP with parameters shown in diagram below. Most exports are GST-free. Once this code is set up you may also want to set up a sale account that has an EXP tax code. Once these two are set up you can continue with the *BASlink* set up and include EXP as part of your G1 and G2.

Diagram 10.9   EXP Tax code setup parameters example and assigning an export sales account with EXP code

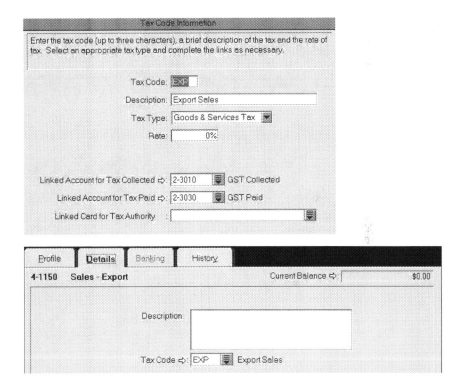

G4 is only relevant if you make input-taxed sales such as financial supplies, existing residential premises and residential rents. If you do make these supplies, you need to set up an Input-taxed sales tax code plus set up a sale account with this new tax code that you just set up. Then continue the setup in you *BASlink* for G4. Below are the screen prints of the new tax code called ITS or input-taxed sales and also the sales – input-taxed account with tax code ITS.

Diagram 10.10 ITS Tax code setup parameters example and assigning an input-taxed sales account with an ITS code

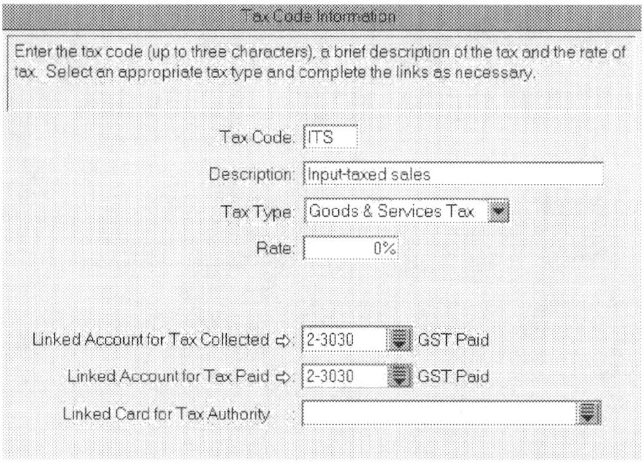

Tax Code Information

Enter the tax code (up to three characters), a brief description of the tax and the rate of tax. Select an appropriate tax type and complete the links as necessary.

Tax Code: ITS
Description: Input-taxed sales
Tax Type: Goods & Services Tax
Rate: 0%

Linked Account for Tax Collected: 2-3030 GST Paid
Linked Account for Tax Paid: 2-3030 GST Paid
Linked Card for Tax Authority:

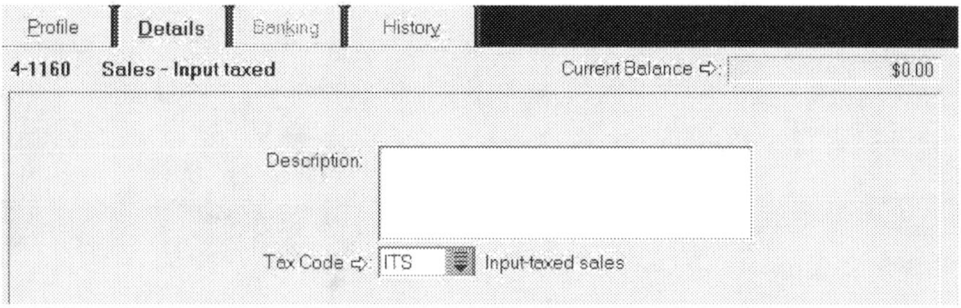

Profile | **Details** | Banking | History

4-1160   Sales - Input taxed   Current Balance: $0.00

Description:

Tax Code: ITS Input-taxed sales

Diagram 10.11 GST worksheet BAS in MYOB as part of *BASlink* setup

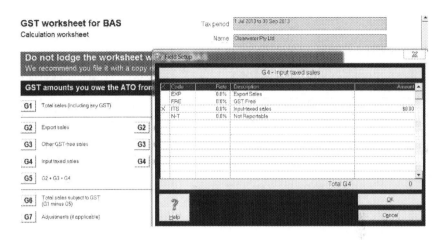

You cannot charge GST for input-taxed supplies. In addition, you are not entitled to input tax credits for the GST paid on the items/services you acquired to make the supply.

G10 should include those with tax code CAP. All purchases other than CAP that are recorded in G10 should be recorded in G11. All purchases that do not have GST included in the price are included in G14. You may set up sales adjustments and purchases adjustments accounts for G7 and G18 but they are generally not used in practice because the sales shown on G1 are already net of adjustments and purchases on G10, G11, G13 and G14 are already net of adjustments. The same is true for G15. This is because the transactions that are recorded into you accounting system like MYOB should only be business related. Normally anything that is personal is recorded in Drawings, Owner Introduced Funds, Advances or Loans to associates that have a tax code of N-T (not taxable). Those transactions would not be included in G10, G11, G13 and G14 anyway so there is really nothing to adjust with.

The correct setup of *BASlink* already puts you in a very good position towards achieving an efficient process with your BAS compliance. When the time comes to lodge you BAS you will have minimal reconciliation to do.

Having a separate reconciliation template in a spreadsheet provides a second check outside MYOB that can be used to ensure that what you lodged so far still match what is in MYOB. This template is available for download from www.accountsunplugged.com

Lodging your BAS online gives you extra time to rather than the normal quarterly cut-off dates of 28 February, 28 April, 28 July and 28 October. Check the ATO website as they release annual concessional dates for BAS lodgement or BAS agents. For the year 2013-14, the following are the concessional dates when you lodge your BAS online via the BAS agent portal, Electronic Commerce Interface (ECI) or Standard Business Reporting (SBR). Note that the October – December quarter BAS is due on the February 28 the following year. This is already an extended cut-off date that is why concession is not available.

Quarter	Standard due dates	Concessional dates
April – June 2013	28 July 2013	25 August 2013
July - September 2013	28 October 2013	25 November 2013
October - December 2013	28 February 2014	Not applicable
January – March 2014	28 April 2014	26 May 2014

If you need more time to prepare and lodge your BAS ring the ATO and request for an extension. Depending on your reason and your circumstances, the ATO may or may not grant extension. With online accounting these days becoming easier and affordable, you will be able to keep on top of your accounts and not spend too much time on them. Many business owners worry about their compliance but they do not actually do something about it.

Please note however that for those that lodge the BAS monthly, concessional dates do not apply, except for the December monthly BAS which is due 21 February the following year instead of 21 January. This only concession for the monthly BAS is available only for small businesses with turnover up to $10 million that report GST monthly and lodge electronically through a registered agent. If the due date falls on a weekend or public holiday you can lodge the form and make payment due on the next business day.

To correct a mistake on your BAS depends on the nature of the mistake. You can use the current BAS to correct GST and fuel tax credit mistakes. You can also vary your PAYG instalment on your current BAS. With PAYG withholding, the original BAS needs to be amended. The amendment process can easily be done online by selecting the BAS that you have lodged and there will be an option called *Request Revision*. Just click that button and follow the steps to put in your new figures. This can easily be done by your BAS agent. If you did not withhold an amount from a payment when it should have been, you need to contact the ATO on 13 28 66. Please note that there are time limits to correct earlier BAS errors in your current BAS based on the turnover of the business summarised below. If the turnover and time limit are not met, the original BAS needs to be amended and interest charges may apply. Also note that the term debit error used by the ATO means the amount owed to them and it is net of credit errors (amount owed to you).

Diagram 10.16 GST error limit thresholds

GST turnover	Error value limit	Time limit
Less than $20m	Less than $10,000	The debit error must be corrected on a BAS that is lodged **within 18 months** of the due date of the BAS in which the error was made.
$20m to less than $100m	Less than $20,000	The debit error must be corrected on a BAS that is lodged **within 12 months** of the due date of the BAS in which the error was made.
$100m to less than $500m	Less than $40,000	The debit error must be corrected on a BAS that is lodged **within 12 months** of the due date of the BAS in which the error was made.
$500m to less than $1b	Less than $80,000	The debit error must be corrected on a BAS that is lodged **within 12 months** of the due date of the BAS in which the error was made.
$1b or more	Less than $450,000	The debit error must be corrected on a BAS that is lodged **within 12 months** of the due date of the BAS in which the error was made.

Refunds and credits including fuel tax can only be claimed within four years from the end of the tax period the credit arose. In the case of excise on imported goods, it is from the date of importation.

To correct mistakes relating to wine equalisation tax (WET) or luxury car tax (LCT), a revised BAS needs to be lodged. A mistake is something that you reported on the BAS that was not correct at all at the time you lodged it. With LCT, adjustments can be made in the current BAS. Adjustments can either be increasing or decreasing.

A mistake occurs if the amount you reported on your activity statement was not correct at the time you lodged your activity statement.

Fuel tax credits

You can correct mistakes and adjust your fuel tax credits on your current activity statement, unless you are outside the correction limits. If so, you will need to revise the earlier activity statement.

Luxury car and wine equalisation taxes

To correct a mistake relating to wine equalisation tax (WET) or luxury car tax (LCT), you need to lodge a revised activity statement. You can make an adjustment to LCT on your current activity statement.

Pay as you go (PAYG) instalments

How you change the PAYG instalment amount you have reported on your activity statement depends on whether your income tax return for that year has been assessed.

Pay As You Go (PAYG) instalment system for expected income tax liability. The income can either be from business or investments. At the end of the year when your income is assessed, the amount you have paid to date will be credited to your tax liability to work out if there's a refund or more tax owing. The ATO uses your previous tax return to estimate tax liability. Generally those who earn $2000 or more will be notified of the instalment unless the latest notice of assessment is less than $500; or if the notional tax is less than $250; or if you are entitled to a senior's or pensioner's tax offset. Companies get notified if their instalment rate is more than 0%; or if notional tax is more than $250. Those companies that have $2 million in business and investment income pay using the instalment rate option.

When the ATO calculates the estimate tax liability it takes into account the likely growth in your business and investment income based on the GDP. The ATO will advise you how often you will make the payments on your BAS.

When transferring figures from your BAS worksheet to the actual Business Activity Statement (BAS) either on paper or online, ensure that you also complete other fields that are required. For example if you lodge by paper you also need to write the name of the person who completed the form and the contact number at the top right of the BAS. When you lodge online you would have already set up your AUSkey credentials under your name so there is no need to put your name on the form. You also need to put the estimated time taken to complete the BAS which includes the time to collect information for the BAS – this is whether you lodge online or by paper. Do not forget to sign and date the BAS form when you lodge by paper. When you lodge online it will ask for your AUSkey password to reconfirm that you are lodging the BAS. Once it is lodged it will give a receipt number. Save or print this page with the receipt number. Create a folder where you save all your BAS-related work. For example, if you are doing your July-September 2013 quarter BAS, name your folder *July-September 2013 BAS*.

If you use Xero online accounting software, print out the Activity Statement report via ***Reports>Activity Statement***

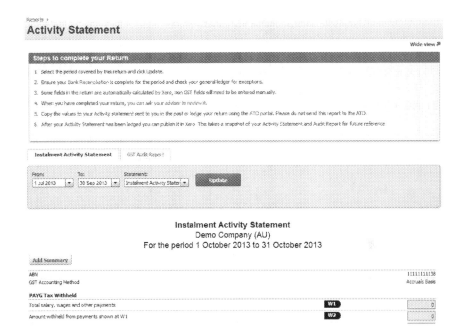

Reports >
Activity Statement

Wide view

Steps to complete your Return

1. Select the period covered by this return and click Update.
2. Ensure your Bank Reconciliation is complete for the period and check your general ledger for exceptions.
3. Some fields in the return are automatically calculated by Xero, non GST fields will need to be entered manually.
4. When you have completed your return, you can ask your advisor to review it.
5. Copy the values to your Activity statement sent to you in the post or lodge your return using the ATO portal. Please do not send this report to the ATO.
6. After your Activity Statement has been lodged you can publish it in Xero. This takes a snapshot of your Activity Statement and Audit Report for future reference.

Instalment Activity Statement	GST Audit Report

From:	To:	Statement:	
1 Jul 2013	30 Sep 2013	Instalment Activity Statement	**Update**

Instalment Activity Statement
Demo Company (AU)
For the period 1 October 2013 to 31 October 2013

Add Summary

ABN		11111111138
GST Accounting Method		Accruals Basis

PAYG Tax Withheld

Total salary, wages and other payments	W1	0
Amount withheld from payments shown at W1	W2	0

Diagram 10.17   Changing the *'From'* and *'To'* dates for your BAS in Xero and click Update

Business Activity Statement
Demo Company (AU)
For the period 1 July 2013 to 30 September 2013

Add Summary

ABN		11111111138
GST Accounting Method		Accruals Basis
Goods and Services Tax (Option 1)		
Total sales	G1	35,674
Does the amount shown at G1 include GST		Yes
Export sales	G2	0
Other GST-free sales	G3	0
Capital purchases (including any GST)	G10	1,375
Non-capital purchases (including GST)	G11	10,651
PAYG Tax Withheld		
Total salary, wages and other payments	W1	0
Amount withheld from payments shown at W1	W2	0
Amount withheld where no ABN is quoted	W4	0
Other amounts withheld (excluding any amount shown in W2 or W4)	W3	0
Total amounts withheld (W2 + W4 + W3)	W5	0
PAYG Income Tax Instalment (Option 1)		
Instalment (copy from BAS)	T7	0
If varying this amount, complete T8, T9 and T4.		
Estimated tax for the year	T8	0
Varied amount for the quarter	T9	0
Reason code for variation list of codes	T4	
Amounts you owe the Tax Office		
GST on sales	1A	3,243
PAYG tax withheld	4	0
PAYG tax income tax instalment	5A	0
Deferred company/fund instalment	7	0

Diagram 10.18 Xero's Activity Statement Report includes a GST Audit report that details the transactions that have GST and GST-free transactions. This is quite handy when you review transactions for the quarter

Notes

Notes

Chapter 11

Important resources and websites

In summary, there are eight steps you need to do to get yourself ready to manage your own books and prepare your own BAS:

1. Print the checklists in Chapters 6 (*Common GST errors*), 9 (*Daily, weekly, monthly, quarterly and yearly tasks*) and 10 (*BAS labels what to include and what not to include*).
2. Make copies of the GST worksheet mailed to you by the ATO. You can also print it from www.ato.gov.au. Print the sample BAS (front and back) below.
3. Print the list of food items that are GST-free in Chapter 2.
4. If you use XERO, make use of the free DEMO version. Take time in setting up your accounts. If in doubt, contact Xero support and check the online forum community.
5. If you use MYOB, take time to set up the *BASlink* and its components. Please refer to Chapter 10.
6. If you use a manual system, work towards moving into either MYOB or Xero online accounting. Spend an hour two every week to familiarise yourself with the functionalities. Xero online free DEMO version is the best place to start.
7. Sign up for AUSkey on https://abr.gov.au and set up your credentials for your Business Portal so you will be able to lodge your BAS online.
8. Go the following website and make them your favourites on your internet browser:

- www.ato.gov.au (Australian Taxation Office for your taxation queries) 13 28 66
- www.fairwork.gov.au (For questions relating to paying employees) 13 13 94
- www.sba.ato.gov.au (ATO's search tool)
- www.dropbox.com (storage website)
- www.accountsunplugged.com (our website for online BAS accountant and various resources)

Below is an example of a Business Activity Statement from the ATO. This is the same as the one shown in Chapter 10.

REPRODUCED from Chapter 10: Diagram 10.1a Example of a quarterly Business Activity Statement (front) from www.ato.gov.au

FRONT

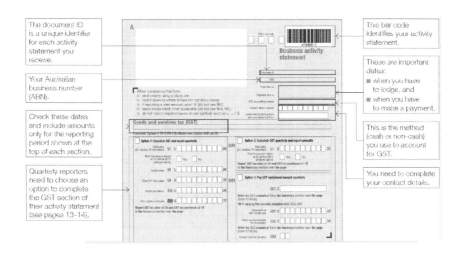

REPRODUCED from Chapter 10: Diagram 10.1b (back)

Example of a quarterly Business Activity Statement (back) from www.ato.gov.au

BACK

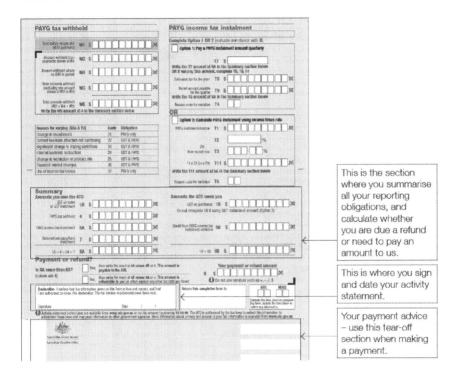

Familiarise yourself with the standard BAS form both front and back pages. Allocate 20 minutes every day for 21 days to go through the items included under each BAS label in Chapter 10 that are applicable to your business. Skill is enhanced by repetition. Although you only spend a few minutes on something as long as you do it consistently you will eventually develop a skill.

You will notice that the sample GST calculation worksheet below from the Australian Taxation Office has more labels than the actual BAS form. This is because the worksheet has subtotals and adjustments as you work through the various labels for your BAS. These labels are included in Chapter 10.

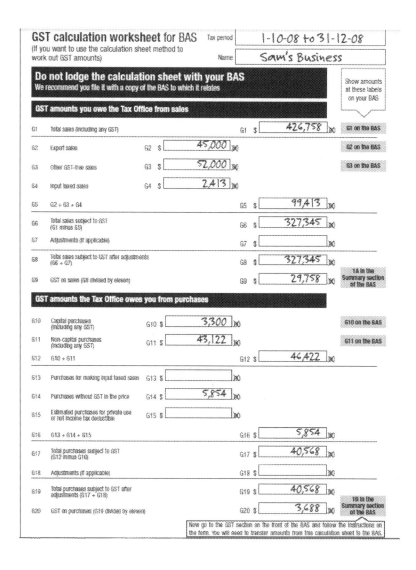

REPRODUCED from Chapter 10: Diagram 10.2 Example of a GST calculation worksheet from www.ato.gov.au

At the end of the year you also need to ensure that your quarterly amounts are reconciled with your total annual amounts on your

Profit and Loss statement and Balance Sheet. For example the total sales on your BAS for the four quarters during the year excluding GST match your total sales on your Profit and Loss statement at the end of the year.

We value your feedback.
Please email to admin@accountsunplugged.com
or visit www.accountsunplugged.com